MW01125701

ENGLAND
AND INDIA

PEOPLE AT ODDS

THE BALKANS: PEOPLE IN CONFLICT

ENGLAND AND INDIA

INDIA AND PAKISTAN

THE IRA AND ENGLAND

ISRAEL AND THE ARAB WORLD

NATIVE AMERICANS AND THE UNITED STATES

PEOPLE AT ODDS

ENGLAND AND INDIA

Jennifer Breen

Chelsea House Publishers
Philadelphia

CHELSEA HOUSE PUBLISHERS

EDITOR IN CHIEF Sally Cheney
DIRECTOR OF PRODUCTION Kim Shinners
CREATIVE MANAGER Takeshi Takahashi
MANUFACTURING MANAGER Diann Grasse

Staff for ENGLAND AND INDIA

ASSISTANT EDITOR Susan Naab
PICTURE RESEARCHER Sarah Bloom
PRODUCTION ASSISTANT Jaimie Winkler
COVER AND SERIES DESIGNER Keith Trego
LAYOUT 21st Century Publishing and Communications, Inc.

http://www.chelseahouse.com

First Printing

1 3 5 7 9 8 6 4 2

Library of Congress Cataloging-in-Publication Data

Breen, Jennifer.
   England and India / Jennifer Breen.
      p. cm. — (People at odds)
Includes bibliographical references (p.) and index.
   ISBN 0-7910-6708-4
   1. Great Britain—Foreign relations—India—Juvenile literature.
2. India—Foreign relations—Great Britain—Juvenile literature. 3. England
—Relations—India—Juvenile literature. 4.India—Relations—England—
Juvenile literature. I. Title. II. Series.
DA47.9.I4 B74 2002
327.42054—dc21

                                                                    2002001306

CONTENTS

1 Britain's Emergence into India   **7**

2 From Traders to King Makers: **30**
    The Formation of an Empire
    Within an Empire

3 The British Conquering of India   **50**

4 The Westernization of India   **72**

5 A Bridge to Freedom   **82**

6 The Road to Independence   **100**

Chronology   **118**

Further Reading   **121**

Resources   **122**

Index   **124**

Britain's Emergence into India

In the last decade of the 15th century, all of western Europe had designs for Asian trade, most specifically with the Asian trading power of India. Western Europe was in the midst of a time of enlightenment called the Renaissance. During this period people looked beyond the previously prescribed classical and orthodox theories; they desired to discover cultures beyond their immediate surroundings. The deterioration of medieval feudalism gave way to a new merchant middle class that sought out new and adventurous business enterprises. These merchants were fascinated by the stories of mystical India, a land of tremendous opportunity.

However, travel to India was very difficult. It was a long and tumultuous land journey. Even greater difficulties were presented by ocean travel, partially due to the popular theory that the world was flat, and rumors of sea monsters in the waters beyond Europe. The merchants and some monarchs

Shown here is a map of Asia. India is located in the south central part of the continent.

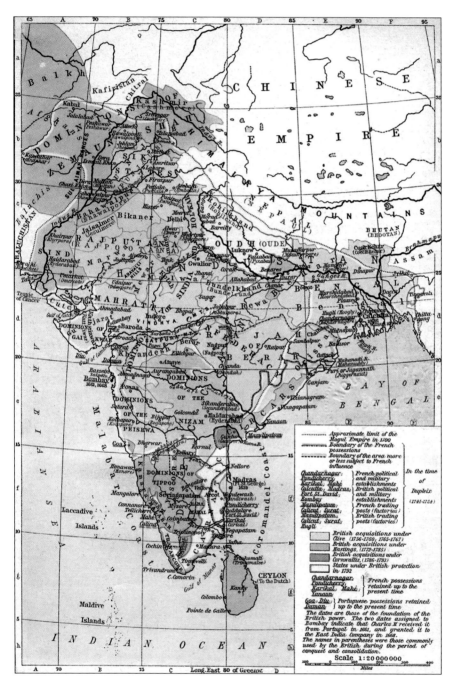

Shown here is a map of India during British and French occupation, before the division of India and Pakistan.

sought a profitable Asian sea route. Christopher Columbus, determined to prove that the world was round, and undeterred by sea monsters, sailed the *Pinta,* the *Niña,* and the *Santa María* in 1492 to seek an easier sea route to India for purposes of exploration and a Spanish trading relationship. He did prove that the world is round, but he did not reach India. Columbus instead made the European discovery of the Americas; but he was so convinced that he landed in India, he called the Native Americans Indians. Columbus's historic voyage also gave birth to the European India trade race. The Portuguese navigator Vasco da Gama quickly followed suit in Columbus's pursuits and in 1497 found an effective route to India around the Cape of Good Hope. In the early 1500s, the Portuguese formed the Estado da India, the first European trade company in India. The Estado da India focused on the trade of Indonesian spices. Throughout the 16th century the Portuguese held an Indian spice monopoly throughout Europe.

THE FORMATION OF THE EAST INDIA COMPANY

Naturally, English merchants also desired a solid trading presence in India. The English did not effectively seek trade permission for India until the beginning of the 17th century. The success of the Portuguese made a trading presence in India highly desirable. The English Elizabethan period was the appropriate time for this trade expansion. The Elizabethan era embodied the Renaissance ideals for England. It was a time of restoration after great political and religious chaos that blossomed into a flourishing of the arts, philosophy, military ventures, exploration, and colonization. The English had developed a sense of nationalist pride during this era that instilled a desire to take action for self-improvement and the betterment of Britain. British emergence into India began on

December 31, 1600, when Queen Elizabeth I decided to grant a private company a fifteen-year royal charter for the purpose of Indonesian trade. A group of English merchants formed the East India Company, and a hefty royal loan of £70,000 helped them to procure the support of wealthy and powerful stockholders. The company continued to renew their royal charters, under new rulers who also gave royal concessions.

The East India Company was made up of two different sectors, with very different roles. The stockholders made up one section of the company. They were the decision-making and financial sector of the East India Company. They operated from the company's offices on Leandenhall Street in London. The other sector of the East India Company was the company men. They performed the on-site trading and diplomatic work for the company. They also worked as the company's military regiment.

The East India Company had a large number of stockholders, numbering close to 2,000. In a way, these stockholders made up the government of the company. They held meetings in parliamentary form. They voted on the most important decisions for the company, such as choosing the directors for the company, constructing policies, designing the company's framework, selecting trading venues, formulating diplomatic plans and government relations, and they undertook all financial determinations and management. The stockholders were men of wealth and political power. In fact, the price of stock required one to be of wealthy standing. "The Company deliberately encouraged holdings of more than £500, which qualified the shareholders to a vote at the annual meeting at its headquarters in Leandenhall Street for the election of the directors." The company immediately had political power, because of the standing of its stockholders, but it became even more powerful after their financial trading successes. At one time the company's stockholders even decided to lend the

As representatives of not only the East India Company but also Britain, employees of the company were expected to be skilled in both trade and diplomacy. It was at trading posts like this one, in Surat, where they carried out their duties.

British government a million pounds. "A Company which could lend money to the government and whose investors carried political clout was well placed to procure political favours." This political power made the stockholders able to continually retain the East India Company's status as a British trading monopoly. They disposed of attempts made by other British trading groups seeking to establish Indian trade.

The other sector of the East India Company, the company men, performed the hands-on work of the trade business. Employment with the East India Company was seen as an honorable profession that would build formidable character and could create wealth. The fortune-seeking, younger sons of many middle- and upper-class families sought positions with the company. The younger sons needed to seek employment because, according to a long-standing English law that began in medieval times, only the oldest son was entitled to the family's holdings. The younger sons were forced to find their way in the world. The traveling tales of the East India Company carried marvelous reputations of adventures and riches that were a very enticing form of recruitment for many young men.

The East India Company demanded many requirements of its company men, and they needed to pass through a series of stages. The men had to have their way to India partially paid and were responsible for many of their own supplies. Therefore, many workers needed to attain sponsorship. They underwent a training course that taught them skills of diplomacy and trading policies. They also studied books written by company directors. The workers were expected to act in a gentlemanly manner at all times, because in a sense they were representatives of not only the company but also of Britain. The men were not immediately entitled to attain "fortunes." The workers had to go through a company process of several stages, to ultimately gain both personal and company success. "First, the Company's employee undertook what was in effect a five-year apprentice-ship as a writer, and then moved up the ladder to become successively a factor, . . . a councillor, and finally, a governor. Salaries were not high, but men holding senior posts were free to trade on their own account." A large amount of revenue could be made by personal trade.

The East India Company also employed many Indians, who worked in the factories and regiments, and assisted in trade. They worked hand in hand with the company men as part of a team. They helped the company men adjust to the Indian culture, climate, and trading policies. The company men and Indian workers had a mutual influence upon each other. They invented many new terms combining English and Indian words, thus constructing a unique company vocabulary. Many

Indian workers gained an interest in the European cultures, while many company men dressed in Indian garments. The company men enjoyed many aspects of this newly learned Indian culture, which led some to marry Indian women.

THE ESTABLISHMENT OF A TRADE RELATIONSHIP BETWEEN THE EAST INDIA COMPANY AND THE INDIAN MUGHAL EMPIRE

The first mission of the East India Company after receiving a royal charter and establishing itself as a company was to create a trading relationship with India. In order to begin trading, it needed to gain the permission of Akbar, the reigning Mughal emperor of India.

In 1600, India was estimated to have a population of 140 million people, while the British Isles had 5 million, and the entirety of western Europe not quite 40 million. The Mughal emperor Akbar ruled over India's population of 100 million people in 1600. The remaining 40 million represented people in either remote areas or small independent principalities. Akbar, who was Muslim, kept order in his empire by incorporating Hindus, who made up the majority of the population, in different positions in government and the military. He dropped a poll tax that had been previously enforced on non-Muslims, and kept aspects of Islam from political life. However, he retained Muslim support by being in the direct line of Muhammad, which, it was believed, made him destined to rule. The Mughal emperor also did not seek to convert his subjects. Akbar even married a Hindu princess. He also attempted to form a religion that united all of the major aspects of India's major religious groups: Hinduism, Islam, Sikhism, Jainism, Buddhism, Zoroastrianism, Judaism, and Christianity. Akbar's openness and awareness of the cultural and religious diversity of India led to the forming of these liberal policies, which were the glue that held his empire together. The population was

organized under a previously installed form of Indian feudalism. His son and grandson followed his polices, and India
experienced a long time of peace.

The East India Company sent representatives to Akbar's
court between 1601 and 1603. The visiting diplomats did
not understand the Mughal emperor. Akbar's court was
spectacular and its wealth was astounding. The European
visitors were greatly impressed by the splendor of his court,
"the eye-catching profusion of solid gold and chased silver,
precious silks and brocades, massive jewels, priceless carpets,
. . . probably without parallel in history." The company's
diplomats mistook Akbar for a despot because of his wealth,
vast rule, and India's feudalism; it was the European assumption
of the time that Asia was comprised of despotic rulers. However, he was not a despot. He embraced what were considered
to be many liberal and humane polices, and like the European
Renaissance kings, he was a great patron of the arts. His court
was filled with musicians, dancers, and artisans.

This misunderstanding concerning the Mughal emperor led
to poor diplomacy. The representatives were also very eager to
trade, having witnessed the displays of Akbar's jewelry and his
palace. The gold and silver of the palace excited them, because
it had all been attained by trade. India itself was not a natural
source of these valuable metals. "India had long been 'an abyss
for gold and silver', drawing to itself the world's bullion and
then nullifying its economic potential by melting and spinning
the precious metals into bracelets, brocades and other ostenta-
tious heirlooms." The notions of Akbar's politics and the
presence of wealth amassed by trade led the diplomats on an
aggressive campaign. They did not merely request trading
privileges but, because their excitement pushed their campaign
too quickly, demanded trading bases and a privilege-granting
farman. A *farman* is an agreement that would release the
company from trade restrictions. Akbar granted them

permission to limited trading, but their aggression made him doubt their assertions of goodwill. He decided it was best for the East India Company to begin their Indian trading activities slowly. Therefore, he did not grant them trading bases or a *farman.*

THE INDIAN PRODUCT AND TRADE

The East India Company originally intended to simply imitate the Portuguese Indonesian spice trade, but it soon found that there was a large market for many different Indian products. The company decided to experiment with the trading of other Indian goods. People in Britain and the rest of western Europe were highly intrigued by the exotic goods. There was soon an obsessive demand for the highly fashionable Indian imports. Some of the most popular items were wall hangings, tea, molasses, different kinds of cloth—taffeta, calico, silk, and chintz—and fine china. The expansion of Indian products beyond the Portuguese spice-focused markets gave the British a lucrative advantage. The popularity of these items brought the company quick success and made their stock valuable and desirable.

The acquiring of Indian goods was a very expensive form of trade. The Mughal emperor and the Indian merchants would only accept gold and silver. The Mughal Empire used the metals gained from trade to print rupees, the Indian currency. The shipping of the goods was also very expensive. However, even with all of these expenses, the Indian products were in such demand that the company was still able to make an incredible profit. This was especially so in Britain and its colonies, because the company held a trade monopoly. Eventually, Britain began to accumulate the majority of its gold and silver from its American colonies. This worked to the advantage of the company, because Indian products were also very popular in the colonies. The British colonies usually followed the trends of Britain, so this made the company's access to these metals easier.

The East India Company assumed that it would also be able to sell a large amount of British and other European products to the Indians, especially English cloth. However, when it embarked on this trade, it was surprised to find that the Indians had little interest in British and other European goods, especially cloth. Among the few things that gathered interest were European weapons and magnifying glasses. The Indians were well experienced in trade and had long been a powerful Asian trading force. The differences in culture, the craftsmanship of their own region, and trade availability left little interest for European goods. Nevertheless, the East India Company suffered no significant financial damage.

SUCCESSFUL TRADE NEGOTIATIONS WITH THE MUGHAL EMPIRE

Salim, the son of Akbar, began his reign in 1605. He took the name Jahangir, meaning "world conqueror." He followed the liberal policies of his father, which made him a successful and unifying ruler over his people. In 1611 he married Nur Jahan ("light of the world"), and at times they co-ruled. Jahangir was also a great patron of the arts, especially painting. When he took the throne, the East India Company became eager to reopen trade negotiations.

The East India Company's initial attempt proved disastrous. It again misjudged the character of the Mughal emperor and made the mistake of sending William Hawkins, the captain of one of its vessels, *The Hector.* The sea captain was an inappropriate choice: his brashness and general lack of diplomatic courtesy offended Jahangir to the point that he did not even renew the company's trading rights granted by his father. After several refusals, Hawkins was replaced by Sir Thomas Roe. The East India Company had finally taken the Mughal emperor more seriously: Roe was a member of the court of King James I and much more skilled in diplomacy. He was an appropriate

Salim, the son of Akbar, began his reign in 1605 and took the name Jahangir, or "World Conqueror." Jahangir's accession to the throne meant another opportunity for the East India Company to win greater trading rights in India.

and a successful choice. He became the ambassador of Britain and the East India Company. He was the East India Company's best representative to the Mughal Empire.

Sir Thomas Roe greatly missed the court of King James I but quickly became acclimated to the court of Jahangir. His prejudices were altered by the grandeur of Jahangir and his court. "Sir Thomas Roe, an emissary from James I of England and a man usually more obsessed with his own dignity, was frankly amazed when he saw Jahangir in ceremonial attire. The emperor's belt was of gold, his buckler and sword 'sett all over with great diamonds and rubyes'." Roe was even more impressed by Jahangir's gallery of paintings, and he claimed that it greatly surpassed that of England's King James I.

Jahangir enjoyed Roe's company and his place in the court. The polite diplomacy was appreciated. Jahangir granted Roe and the company trading rights throughout his empire. In 1611, Jahangir gave the company permission to establish a trading base in Machilipatnam, and in 1619 he gave the company permission to establish a factory in Surat. Owing to his diplomatic success, Roe sought to gain an imperial *farman* from Jahangir. A *farman* would release the company from many trade restrictions and set it ahead of newly emerging European competitors. Roe could not, however, persuade Jahangir to bestow a *farman* on the company. Jahangir did not feel that it was in the best interest of the empire or India's own trading industry to give the company a *farman*.

BRITISH-MUGHAL TRADE NEGOTIATIONS REACH A STANDSTILL

Jahangir was succeeded by his son Khurram in 1627, who took the name Shah Jahan, meaning "king of the world." Shah Jahan continued the tradition of liberal policy, and, owing to his own and the land expenditures of past emperors, the Mughal Empire reached the height of centralized rule during his reign. More than 26 million men were now employed as a reserve military force in his army. He also continued patronage of the arts, and his focus was on the growth of architecture. Shah Jahan is responsible for the construction of the Taj Mahal and the city of Shahjahanabad, later known as Old Delhi.

Even though he followed many of his father's and grand-father's policies, Shah Jahan held an indifference to British trade policy negotiations. During the end of Jahangir's reign, Sir Thomas Roe was fearful of negotiations with Shah Jahan. "If he [Prince Khurram, the future Shah Jahan] should offer me ten [forts] I would not accept one,' he told the factors, '. . . for without controversy it is an errour to affect garrisons and land warrs in India. . . . Let this be received as a rule, that if you will profitt, seek it at sea and in quiett trade.'" Roe felt that the only way Shah Jahan would grant the company continued trade permission would be if the company gave him military aid, because of the expansion of his empire. Roe believed, however, it would be a great mistake to make such a bargain. An involvement in internal Indian battles could prove fatal to trade. The East India Company agreed; they did not wish to give military aid for trade advancement. They did not make the same efforts of diplomacy during Shuh Jahan's reign as they had in the past. Also, Shah Jahan felt that a *farman* could be detrimental to India's trade and would not grant a *farman* under any circumstances.

THE SEIZURE OF MADRAS

Since there was no possibility of a *farman* or advancement under Shah Jahan, the East India Company decided to act upon its own accord. The company acquired Madras from its local *nayak,* an independent ruler, through stages of bribery, coercion, and skirmishes in a campaign from 1639 to 1640. In 1641, the company erected Fort St. George, Madras, as a trading base. Even though the company did not get imperial permission for this action, they did not receive repercussions from Shah Jahan because Madras was outside of the Mughal Empire.

A TIME OF TURBULENCE AND OPPORTUNITY

In 1658, Shah Jahan fell ill and his crown was challenged by four of his sons. The two front-runners for the throne were Dara Shikoh, the eldest son, who was the assigned heir and member of the court; and the younger son, Aurangzeb, who was a military governor in Deccan and favored by orthodox Muslims for his devotion to the faith and because of his brother's lack of interest. The two brothers and their armies went to war, and Aurangzeb attained victory. He then defeated his father's army. Aurangzeb usurped Shah Jahan's crown and imprisoned his father for the remaining eight years of his life. He eventually captured and put Dara Shikoh to death. Aurangzeb would change the face of the Mughal Empire.

Aurangzeb abandoned the liberal policies of the previous rulers and sought to regain India's place in the Islamic world. He was a very devout Muslim, often historically viewed as an extremist. He instilled the law of Sharia, which held the entirety of the Mughal Empire under the strictest Islamic principles. He dismissed the dancers, musicians, and artisans from the court and replaced them with moral officers and judges. He banned gambling, alcohol, opium, and blasphemy. He reissued the *jizya,* a poll tax on non-Muslims that had been released by Akbar. The tax made every non-Muslim male pay, based on earnings, for imperial protection. He did not impose this tax on Muslims because they would be called to arms in the case of a *jihad,* a Muslim holy war. He issued heavy taxes on Hindu merchants, pilgrims, and Brahman temple revenues. A large number of high-level Hindu government and military officials were replaced with Muslims. Hindu temples that had been recently built or reconstructed were ordered to be destroyed and mosques were built in their place. The Sikhs of Punjab fared no better. Aurangzeb was angry with the Sikhs for harboring Dara Shikoh, and shortly after the beginning of his

Aurangzeb, a strict adherent to Islam, abandoned the liberal policies of the previous Mughal rulers. His policies caused trouble not only for non-Muslims but also for the East India Company.

reign, he requested the presence of a Sikh leader in his court. While traveling to Aurangzeb's court, the Sikh leader, Guru Tegh Bahadur, preached throughout the countryside. Aurangzeb became angry when he heard of Muslim conversions; he considered this to be an offense of blasphemy. When Guru Tegh Bahadur reached the imperial court, he was immediately sentenced to death. The peaceful Sikhs were horrified and outraged. Aurangzeb took his new rules very seriously, regardless of circumstance. He sent *muhtasibs,* moral officers, to every region of the empire to ensure his edicts were enforced. This new strict style of rule began to dissolve the glue that had held India's diverse peoples in unity.

Aurangzeb's stringent rule and policies created many enemies throughout the Mughal Empire. His treatment of Hindus and Sikhs caused several small rebellions, and many Muslims were upset by what they considered to be fanaticism. No one, however, was so great an enemy of Aurangzeb as the devout Hindu, Shivaji, and the Marthas of Deccan. The Marthas were mostly Hindu, but they were joined by fighters of many different faiths, including Muslims. The Marthas declared Deccan to be their homeland, independent of Mughal rule, and named Shivaji as their king. Shivaji soon became a popular symbol of independence throughout the empire. Shivaji and the Marthas ravaged Mughal territories as an unstoppable force from the beginnings of Aurangzeb's reign until the death of Shivaji on April 30, 1680.

In 1682 the nearby Deccan sultanates of Mewar and Jodhpur formed an alliance to gain independence. Aurangzeb sent his son, Akbar, to fight them, but much to his surprise, Akbar joined forces with Shivaji's son, Sambhaji, now leader of the Marthas, and declared himself Mughal emperor. Enraged by these actions of insubordination, Aurangzeb declared a jihad and, in 1683, moved his entire court and army from Shahjahanabad to Deccan, thus embarking on a 24-year-long military campaign. By 1689 he was able to reduce the sultanates to submission, chased his son into Persia, and tortured and murdered Sambhaji; but he was held in Deccan for the remainder of his reign by continuous rebellions.

The East India Company's trade and commerce were also greatly affected by the turbulence of Aurangzeb's reign. In

When King Charles II of England married the Portuguese princess Catherine of Braganza, he received the fort at Bombay as part of her dowry. The British Crown leased Bombay to the East India Company and thus made it possible for the company to establish a western trade headquarters.

1664, Shivaji and the Marthas attacked the Mughal holdings in Surat. The company's factory was destroyed, and only their heavily protected fort survived the attack. Then trade was furthered damaged when the Marthas pillaged and destroyed Surat for a second time in 1670.

Not every thing during Aurangzeb's reign was destructive for the East India Company. There was also trade expansion. In 1661, as the result of an British and Portuguese alliance against Dutch traders, the Portuguese fort at Bombay was given to King Charles II as part of the dowry of his bride, the Portuguese princess Catherine of Braganza. After a failed attempt to establish a royal trading presence, the British Crown decided in 1688 to lease Bombay to the company at the price of £10 per year. The company had now established a western trading fort.

Aurangzeb's long military campaign paved the way for many trade opportunities. The attention of the Mughal Empire from 1683 to 1707 was its conflicts in Deccan, which loosened the reins on the rules of trade and weakened India's own trading and shipping industries. European traders could now move beyond many pre-established trading lines. This greatly benefited the East India Company, but even more so their senior officers, who, according to contract, were permitted to engage in independent trade. The men of the East India Company did not make their main profits through company business, but instead through personal trading.

The weakening of India's shipping industry led many independents toward trade through shipping Indian products to other regions. "They owned or leased ships, freighted cargoes, sold insurance, and above all took advantage of the security and protection of their employer's flag." The independents used the benefits of the company's status to ship goods to other places and conduct private trade for personal benefit. An example of a company man representing this type of entrepreneur is the famous Elihu Yale. "Thus from Madras, as employees of the Company, the American-born Yale brothers amassed considerable fortunes in trade with Siam (Thailand) and Canton in China; part of Elihu Yale's earnings would endow the college, and later university, in Connecticut which bears his name." While these independent ventures sometimes hurt the company's prospects as a whole, they were seen as legitimate and were supported and followed rules set by the company. Some independents secretly defected and joined with other European trading companies for personal profit. There were also independent company men known as "interlopers" who financed vessels but did not wish to follow any company's rules, so they disguised their ships and flew flags of other European companies, without affiliation. Often times the dealings of the interlopers led to acts of piracy. These independent movements and defections not only broke the rules of the Mughal Empire but also hurt the company's sense of unity.

CHILD'S WAR

In 1692, during the beginning of Aurangzeb's problems in Deccan, the East India Company decided to take advantage of the situation by beginning a campaign for a tax break and *farman*. The company's director, William Hedges, sought to convince the Mughal governor of Bengal, Shaista Khan, who was considered to have great influence over Aurangzeb, to support the company's plea in the disposal of a tax on imported bullion paid for Indian exports as well as another diplomatic mission to receive an imperial *farman*. Hedges felt he was successful in swaying Shaista Khan, but in 1684 the company was plagued by internal arguments. Shaista Khan was offended by these disputes and deemed the company as unworthy of his favor and influence; he voiced strong opposition against the company, and it was refused the tax break and the *farman*. Angered by this rejection, and feeling they had the advantage of Aurangzeb's distraction, the company decided to act upon a royal edict previously granted by King Charles II allowing it to use force on non-Christians for the extension and protection of trade.

In 1688, the East India Company began what was soon to be known as "Child's War." In a series of strikes led by head officer Child, and continuing into 1689, the company attacked Mughal shipping. The company believed that its trade influence and Aurangzeb's absence in Deccan would mean success. Early in 1689, however, Aurangzeb surprised the company with a large Mughal war fleet. Child and his men were forced to retreat to Bombay Castle, where they were trapped for nearly a year. In 1690 the company sought Aurangzeb's forgiveness. It did not want to lose its trading position in India, so it promised goodwill and peace. Aurangzeb forgave the company and returned its trading rights. He also gave the company permission to settle in Calcutta. Fort William was completed in Calcutta in 1696. The company was not, however, granted a *farman*. Aurangzeb would consider giving it a *farman* only if it would police the Indian waters for piracy. Claiming it could not become involved in Indian politics—even though European traders were responsible for a great deal of the piracy—and that it did not have the military resources, the company refused.

At the beginning of the 18th century, the East India Company was punished for the peace agreements it had made with the Mughal Empire after Child's War. The Martha admiral Kanhoji Angria launched a number of attacks on British shipping. No ship bearing a British flag on India's west coast was safe. The fighting continued until the middle of the century. By the 1730s neither side had proved victorious. Kanhoji Angria, however, after inflicting severe damage on the trading port of Bombay, had made great gains.

THE *FARMAN*

The end of Aurangzeb's rule in 1707 brought tremendous discord to India, owing to the combination of his internal policies, vast military expenditures, and a series of succession crises. While the Mughal Empire still retained power, successor states, or independent principalities, ruled by feudal lords and nawabs, began to rise out of the wreckage. This new India also changed the role and mission of the East India Company.

The East India Company focused on attaining a *farman,*

but now with greater privileges. The Mughal succession crisis seemed to be the perfect opportunity. The company's representative, Governor Thomas Pitt of Fort St. George, Madras, who was also a member of the British Parliament, forged a deal with Aurangzeb's heir, Prince Muazzam, later known as Bahadur Shah. Pitt changed the company's previous policies and promised military aid to help Muazzam attain the throne in the battle against his rivals. In return for the company's military aid, Muzzaam would grant the company an imperial *farman*. Prince Muzzam agreed, however his foe never arrived for battle and he acquired the throne without military force. He became Bahadur Shah and quickly ended talks of a *farman*. Bahadur Shah died three years later, in 1710, and his successor did not live long enough to even make any official proclamations, let alone entertain an British *farman* campaign.

The East India Company was very pleased when Farrukhsiyar began his reign; it had been showering him with gifts and favors since his birth, and it was sure it would gain his instant acceptance of a request for a *farman*. Farrukhsiyar was very fond of the English and immediately renewed their trading rights, but, like the previous emperors, in protection of his empire's interests, he was reluctant to grant the company a *farman*. After continuous campaigns of gifts and diplomacy, Farrukhsiyar still would not give into granting a *farman*. Farrukhsiyar became fearful, however, when the company threatened to completely withdraw all trade from India, and so he decided it was worth the granting of a *farman* in order to maintain the profitability of British trade throughout his empire. On New Year's Eve, 1716, Farrukhsiyar signed an agreement and thus officially granted an imperial *farman*. This was by far the East India Company's largest success so far in India. "In Calcutta, Madras and Bombay celebrations were held, toasts were drunk, and salutes fired as the document was paraded through the streets and proclaimed at the cities' gates: 'Our dear bought *farman*' became the 'Magna Carta of the Company in India.'"

The British had great cause for celebration when they received the *farman*. This document was very meaningful to the East India Company in a number of ways. It gave them many privileges and advantages. The *farman* raised their trading status in India, essentially reforming the company and its mission. It instated the company as an imperial office within the Mughal Empire that would be respected by emerging nawabs and successor states. The *farman* placed the British competitively well above all of the other European trading companies. Indian trade agents now gave East India Company employees priority. "Appreciating the *farman*-enhanced status of the Company and credit-worthiness of its employees, such agents placed a high value on their English clients and readily arranged both their investments and the loans needed to finance them."

The *farman* gave the British traders not only a political and economic edge in India but also the right to expand their military force. After the *farman,* the East India Company made a tremendous expansion in the number of troops and weapons in its arsenal. It also employed many Indians as professional soldiers, known as "sepoys." The *farman* gave the company an extension of military rights for the protection of its interests, and even an entitlement to territory in the event of victory in a dispute. It was also able to lease its troops out in return for territory with taxation. The Mughal Empire gave this concession originally so it could call upon British aid during a time of war, but a difference of interpretation led the East India Company to claim greater military expansion and rights than originally intended. In this way, the East India Company also became a military power.

Britain's emergence into India was not made by a nation

but by an independent, although royally supported, trade company. In 1601, the East India Company entered India as a small group of entrepreneurs seeking spice trade, but product experimentation allowed the company to grow tremendously. Years of negotiation and struggle gained it trading bases and an established trade presence in India. The imperial *farman* granted in 1716 secured the company's status as a major trading force in India. It was now not only a foreign trading company but also an economic and military power in India. The *farman* would further change the company's place and mission in India.

From Traders
to King Makers:
The Formation
of an Empire
Within an Empire

The enhanced status resulting from the granting of the *farman* was the first step in the changed intentions of the East India Company. The breakup of Indian rule into different hands and the consequent divisions furthered the company's increase of power. The dissolution of the Mughal Empire left the company as a formidable force, and its victory in European trade competition led it to bounty and land conquest. The 18th and 19th centuries brought a new European trading presence to India, one that was no longer content with the simple business of trading, but instead sought to master trade by ownership.

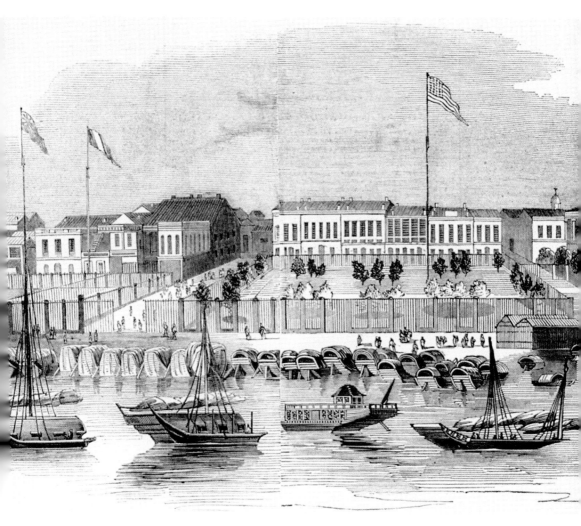

After it was granted a *farman* in 1716, the East India Company began its transformation into not only an economic power but also a political and military one. The illustration shows one of its trading houses in Canton, China.

THE DISSOLUTION OF MUGHAL RULE

The vastness of the Mughal Empire had always required an extremely large army, but it was an economic impossibility to support an army of millions. The majority of the army worked on a reserve basis. The continuous succession crises and military campaigns against the Marthas and against newly emerging rebellions drained the treasury. This left the door open for new principalities to form. The dissolution of the empire and unpaid wages for military services left many soldiers disgruntled. They banded together under their leaders, who decided to take advantage of the damaged empire, living off of the peasantry until they could form their own principalities. The emergence of these warlord principalities only added to the fighting that was prevalent among the small principalities.

The new principalities held respect for the Mughal Empire, and they molded their own states after its example. They never sought to dispel or bring a complete end to the Mughal Empire because of its policy associations with the European traders, and they had rights within India to bestow power.

Even though the principalities did not seek to destroy the Mughal Empire after attaining their freedom, from the 1720s to the 1740s they constantly attacked one another. They sought to increase domination, bounty, and to gain and protect territory. Many times the fighting would be caused by the debts of a previous war. The wars became a continuous cycle of financial need. In order to maintain their small states, the principalities would have to engage in war to pay off the debts to bankers and soldiers from a previous war.

Although the constant fighting created opportunities for the East India Company, it also brought a lot of trouble. The company men faced numerous setbacks and difficulties from the warring princes. It was essential for the company to keep abreast of every political situation that was occurring. Battles affected trade routes. If employees were uninformed, they could easily find themselves in the midst of a battle while transporting products. It was even more important that the company have as much information as possible to prepare for diplomacy with each new principality. Even though the company had an imperial *farman,* which was still enforced and respected by the new principalities, it was still responsible for the payment of trade-related taxes in these newly formed sovereignties. Diplomacy was also more difficult. While the new principalities molded themselves after the Mughal Empire, their diplomacy did not always aspire toward a courtly manner. The Mughal emperors, like the European monarchs, were trained from birth for possible accession to the throne; many of these new rulers in the now-fragmented India were simple men who had answered the call of opportunity. While most of its energies were still spent on the Mughal emperor, the company's diplomatic structure needed now to also include the individual principalities. The company also continually engaged in sea battles around Bombay with the Marthas well into the middle of the 18th century.

The East India Company also answered the challenge of opportunity. During the strong period of the Mughal Empire the East India Company was just a small trading company, but now, in a divided India, it, too, could be an effective military force. The company occasionally leased its Indian sepoys to principalities desperate for soldiers but unable to pay in currency. The reward for the company's help was often a piece of territory in the losing principality and part of the bounty taken during battle. The company's soldiers performed very well because they were professionally trained and had superior weaponry. The company's soldiers were so successful that some superstitious Indian princes even began to dress their soldiers in red garments similar to the East India Company sepoy uniform, hoping that would give them luck in battle. This period of the 1720s–1740s taught the East India Company that fortune could be made not only by trade but also through military aid, resulting in gifts of territory and bounty.

WAR WITH FRANCE

The imperial Mughal *farman,* as well as the demise of the Portuguese in India and the British inheritance of their holdings, ensured the East India Company standing in India as the dominant European trade force, but these factors did not remove the company's European competition. In fact, the dissolution of the Mughal Empire stimulated greater competition, most especially from the late-coming French trading company, Compagnie des Indes. The success of the British *farman* and the opportunity presented by the disso-lution of the Mughal Empire excited and inspired the Compagnie des Indes to seek many new trade endeavors, which brought them a great deal of success since their late appearance in the Indian trade market in the 1660s. In the middle of the 18th century the French company held a close second to the British East India Company in the European trade race.

The French company was very successful in trade but lacked the sort of national and governmental support its British counterpart enjoyed. The Compagnie des Indes received a smaller financial investment from its stock-holders, and the French government showed less interest in Indian trading. Also, the Compagnie did not have the same type of support in France that the East India Company had in Britain because the French public did not hold the same amount of interest in Indian products. The Com-pagnie earned much of its revenue from trade with other countries. The Indian imports were popular with the French aristocracy, but there were peasant and worker revolts against Indian imports. In France, "in some quarters there was hostility to trade with India: the peasantry feared an influx of Indian food, and textile manufacturers protested against imports of cheap Indian fabrics." The French peasantry felt very strongly against trade with India; in fact, there was an instance of a public burning of Indian cloth in Paris. These hostile feelings led the government and potential investors to focus primarily upon the French sugar-producing islands in the Caribbean and the Northern American colonies. The absence of support for Indian trade meant that the Compagnie would have to reach beyond normal trading procedures in order to ever surpass its second-place position in India.

The Compagnie des Indes desired to find a source of revenue that would ensure its success in India. It could not depend on investors or national trade support. The Compagnie sought, therefore, to acquire territory in India, in which capital could be made through taxation. The dissolution of the Mughal Empire made such a plan possible. The Compagnie officials decided that their plan for Indian land seizure would be effective only if they established themselves as a military power in India. The best way to accomplish such a reputation was by defeating their European competitors. The Europeans were already renowned for their military strength in the battles of the principalities, such as demonstrated by the East India Company's sepoys. The most obvious choice was to attack and dethrone the dominant status of the East India Company. The Compagnie's plans for a military strike against the East India Company were made in the fall of 1744, when news arrived from Europe that Britain and France were at war. The commanding French officer, Joseph-François Dupleix, decided, however, it was in the Compagnie's best interest to forge a treaty with the East India Company, because British naval ships were near.

Although the Compagnie was willing to engage in battle with the East India Company, it knew that defeat was certain if the British Royal Navy had involvement. The East India Company was also glad to sign a treaty; they did not wish to engage in a European war in India.

The treaty between the East India Company and the Compagnie des Indes did not last long. The British Royal Navy attacked one of the Compagnie trade ships off the coast of China in September of 1745. Soon after the French began to make military plans against the East India Company. In September 1746, Dupleix led French troops from the Compagnie's headquarters in Pondicherry in a launch of land and sea assaults on the East India Company's holdings in Madras. Dupleix and his troops seized Madras by the end of the month. Shortly after the capture of Madras, 10,000 men—sepoys and troops given for assistance by a local principality—were easily defeated by a few hundred French troops. "It soon became axiomatic that European leadership, soldiers, weaponry and tactics were infinitely superior to Indian." Soon after the French seizure of Madras, a monsoon storm destroyed the Compagnie's fleet, which placed sea power in India back into British favor. The Royal Navy assisted the garrison of Fort St. David and Cuddalore in holding off the French in December of 1746 and March of 1747. The French seizure of Madras made it clear to both the French and the British that battle at sea was the key to winning a war in India. Now that the French fleet had fallen into disrepair, the British dominated this powerful element of war and were prepared to strike the French. The British launched a counter-attack on the Compagnie in Pondicherry in the summer of 1748. Dupleix had nothing with which to face the attacking fleet since the remainder of his warships had been taken in May of 1747. Nonetheless, Pondicherry withstood a seven-day attack by British land and sea forces. Then another monsoon

In the summer of 1747 the British launched a seven-day attack against French-controlled Pondicherry. The French fleet was crippled but the British had also to battle a raging storm at sea.

storm drove away the British ships and troops. In January of 1749 Britain and France signed the Treaty of Aix-la-Chapelle, but, despite the treaty, the fighting in India between the two companies did not end. The treaty focused mainly on the North American colonies and the Caribbean. It did bring a lull in the fighting between the two companies, and the East India Company was able to regain Madras, however this slowdown in fighting did not bring peace between the two companies in India. Instead it inspired a new form of fighting, an indirect fight for domination.

The Compagnie des Indes had suffered great financial losses after the strike on Pondicherry. It faced bankruptcy, and so it decided to move the war to a new front. The fighting could no longer be simply for commercial gain; the Compagnie would move toward land domination in the form of becoming a king maker. It planned the overthrow of principalities and the installation of French puppet rulers. Dupleix soon became the power broker of southern India, and attained a great fortune. The East India Company followed suit. In the earlier stages of the war, many principalities gave allegiance to both sides of the conflict for fear of punishment for noninvolvement. The battle would now be fought solely through principalities and their allegiances. The superior European weaponry made it easy to take principalities, and the French and British justified their actions with the view that the nawabs were unfit rulers. King making proved to be very profitable for both companies: when they would overthrow a principality, the puppet ruler would bestow upon them the bounty as patronage. The two companies now fought for principalities and waged wars between the principalities in the guise of fighting one another. "Henceforth, when not officially at war, British and French could continue their hostilities under the aegis of competing Indian princes. Through these same princes they would extend their authority without seeming to acquire territories."

Hostilities erupted between the companies with their involvement in the Carnatic Wars. The Carnatic Wars began in 1749 and lasted until 1754 and were fought through allied principalities and puppet rulers. The battles began in August 1749, when Dupleix lead Compagnie troops in the overthrow of the nawab of Karnataka, Anwar-ud-Din, and replaced him with the French puppet ruler, Chandra Singh. Dupleix and his men gained much wealth from this venture, but they also attained influence over the key territory in southern India. The territory in Karnataka branched into the East India Company's treasured Madras. The company refused to accept the French puppet rule of Karnataka. It gave its allegiance to the son of the dethroned Anwar-ud-Din, Muhammad Ali, who had been granted a political office. In fear of a coup, Chandra Singh sought to depose Muhammad Ali. In 1751, after the occurrence of many small skirmishes, Chaudra Singh challenged Muhammad Ali and the East India Company to contest himself and the Compagnie des Indes for the rule of Karnataka.

This challenge would bring forth the military devices of the man who was later credited as the English conqueror of India. Robert Clive, much like Dupleix, was a disgruntled younger son who sought fortune and glory in India in order to finally gain the acceptance of a begrudging father. Clive began his service in India as a company clerk at Fort St. George in Madras in June of 1744. Clive had disdain for company clerking duties and desired adventure, like the tales that had recruited him. He dreamed of moving beyond his desk and gaining power. Clive had a special bond and rapport with the Indian workers and learned a great deal from these friendships. This social involvement served as the key to his military successes. Clive was happy when he was able to become enlisted in military ventures for the company. His friendships with the workers gave him a special and different understanding of the sepoys. He was able to examine their psychology and inspire them to fight as no other leader could; he was able to identify with what they held important. He took heavy risks in battle to ignite bravery in his men. His ambition for fame and fortune, and his bond with his troops, made Clive and his army a very dangerous weapon unleashed by the East India Company.

The East India Company decided that the best way to dispose of French rule in Karnataka was to stage a coup in its capital, Arcot. Robert Clive and an army of 800 men surprised an undefended Arcot on September 1, 1751. Having heard about the march of the British through a monsoon storm, the Indian military commander was fearful of the troops. The commander panicked and allowed Clive and his troops to march in and take Arcot and its heavily stocked arsenal with ease. Soon after Clive's victory in Arcot the city was surrounded by 10,000 French troops and their Indian allies. Knowing of Indian war tactics through his close relationships with the sepoys, Clive was able to use some of his enemies' tactics against them. For example, he reversed an attack of elephants that were employed to bring down the city walls. Clive did this by placing a large amount of gunpowder underneath the elephants. Once ignited, the gunpowder exploded, sending the elephants in a panic. In their state of panic, the elephants reversed their direction, and trampled their Franco-Indian masters. Clive and his men withstood 50 days of attack. They also withstood many bribery attempts. On the 50th day, Clive was supplied with reinforcements from company troops and Marthan allies. The company forces went on the offensive, and the exhausted Franco-Indian troops retreated.

The victory at Arcot was very important for the East India Company. "It was a turning point in the fortunes of the British, for it had revealed that the French were not invincible." During the years 1752 and 1753, Clive and the company's commander in chief, Colonel Stringer, continually defeated the French in the pursuit of domination of southern India. After these successful military ventures, Clive returned to England and purchased a fashionable home and made an attempt—which ended in failure—to acquire a seat in the House of Commons. Clive spent his fortune very quickly and so returned to

Led by Robert Clive, the East India Company won an important victory at Arcot over the French. Throughout the early 1750s, the British successfully thwarted French attempts to dominate southern India.

India in 1756 to renew his military employment as the governor of Fort St. David.

The Compagnie des Indes was dissatisfied by its situation in India. Many members of the Compagnie felt that Dupleix had taken too many risks. As governor and commander in chief of the Compagnie des Indes, Dupleix did not feel it was imperative to listen to the stockholders. However, the stockholders, as well as the French government, did not want an accumulation of territory in India. They had authorized fighting only to protect trade and the original outposts needed for trade. They were very angry because the continuous British victories had made it obvious they were entrenched in a conflict they had no chance of winning. The stockholders were not pleased with Dupleix's decisions. In 1752 the Compagnie ordered Dupleix to give his resignation. His tremendous ambition led him to refuse and he kept up his military ventures. Eventually, however, he could no longer avoid resigning and, in 1753, departed from Pondicherry.

The Compagnie sent a replacement for Dupleix, Charles Godeau, whom they sent essentially to end the conflict with the East India Company. In January 1755 Godeau effected a break in the French and British conflicts. The battles between the two companies had been becoming increasingly dangerous. Both had had to appeal for military aid from their home countries. Both companies had also been hiring professional soldiers from other European countries. To further increase their regiments, they had both enlisted untrained men from the slums of London and Paris, and even took men from the prisons. The East India Company led the race and could now dictate trade and political conditions.

The break in the fighting with the French gave the East India Company the opportunity to focus on expansion and greater profits. Combining the roles of conqueror and king maker with trade earned incredible fortunes for some company men. The accumulation of territory and regional influence enabled the company to remove the Indian middlemen from trade. New conquests became highly desirable.

An example of a lucrative conquest is an attack that occurred in 1756, when Clive and Admiral Charles Watson, of the Royal Navy, traveled to Bombay to bring an end to the long-running sea raids by the Marthas. In the course of the fighting, they captured and pillaged the wealthy Marthan fort of Vijaydurg, after which they departed for Madras.

SIRAJ-UD-DAULAH

The desire for conquest left the East India Company distracted. Their methods of diplomacy suffered greatly. Since the 1740s the nawab of Bengal, the largest of the Mughal provinces, had been badly stressed by the financial damage British trade had inflicted upon Bengal. The conflicts with France halted diplomacy, and the company ignored the problems in Bengal. The nawab's heir, Siraj-ud-Daulah, however, desired to remove the British from Bengal and decided to take advantage of the company's distractions.

Siraj-ud-Daulah became the nawab of Bengal in 1756. He was extremely angered by the financial troubles caused by the East India Company and the military threats of their bases. The company forts, built for the purpose of battle with Indians, instilled intimidation. In response to his feelings, Siraj-ud-Daulah launched an attack on the company base at Fort William in Calcutta in July 1756. He was able to take Calcutta with ease, not least because Clive and Watson had their attention focused on the Marthas in Bombay and later on company matters in Madras. Upon taking Calcutta, Siraj-ud-Daulah demanded that the fortifications of Fort William be destroyed, since, despite their alleged protective purposes, they had been built for fighting Indians, and most especially since they could lead to the destruction of Bengal.

THE BLACK HOLE OF CALCUTTA

Siraj-ud-Daulah's taking of Calcutta was soon followed by the infamous story of the "Black Hole of Calcutta." Tales of the Black Hole of Calcutta ran rampant throughout all of India and western Europe. When Siraj-ud-Daulah overtook Fort William, then the prized fort of the East India Company, rumors had it that he imprisoned British inhabitants in an underground, airless dungeon overnight. In the morning, when his guards went to check the prisoners, most had died of suffocation. The story of the Black Hole of Calcutta was originally recounted by the English survivor John Zephaniah Holwell. His embellished account claimed that 146 people were imprisoned in a very small chamber, and 123 perished. Many accounts of this story were published and distributed. However, scholars have proven that there could not have been more than 69 people imprisoned. It was later proven that Siraj-ud-Daulah had no part in this incident. He did not order the imprisonment. Many scholars argue whether or not the incident ever really happened.

The Black Hole of Calcutta sealed the fate of Siraj-ud-Daulah and Bengal. Siraj-ud-Daulah was universally blamed for the deaths. The British looked upon him as being a cruel, deceptive, and cowardly despot. When news of the incident reached Clive in Madras, he vowed to take revenge on Siraj-ud-Daulah, even beyond retaking Calcutta.

A few months later, Clive and Watson and the company's troops were able to retake Calcutta with ease. It was not difficult for the company to regain Calcutta, because Siraj-ud-Daulah had not made this move for expansion but for his demands to be heard. However, Clive was not content with simply taking back Calcutta; he desired to further punish Siraj-ud-Daulah by dethroning him and installing a favorable political surrogate in Bengal.

THE BATTLE OF PLASSEY

Clive set forth in a carefully planned coup to depose Siraj-ud-Daulah. He convinced Mir Jafar, the granduncle of Siraj-ud-Daulah, to join with the company. Clive promised to enthrone Jafar as the nawab of Bengal. Clive also persuaded many of Siraj-ud-Daulah's leading military officers and their troops by bribery to many acts of treason. Clive forged many documents that enabled him to carry out this secret coup undetected.

On June 23, 1757 Clive led company troops to face Siraj-ud-Daulah's army at the village of Plassey, midway between Calcutta and Murshidabad. The company's victory had been decided before the two forces approached the battlefield. The surprised Siraj-ud-Daulah had been abandoned by Jafar's troops, whose alliance had been promised. Many of the troops that were present were bribed. They surrendered to the company very early and unleashed attacks upon Siraj-ud-Daulah. Bengal's army fell defeated, and a few days later the missing Siraj-ud-Daulah's body was found in a nearby river. The Battle of Plassey, not acknowledged as a battle of great military magnitude in its time, was later credited with beginning the British domination in India.

Clive and the company troops pillaged Bengal. Then they had Jafar, the new ruler, open the vaults of the rich Bengal to Clive and the company men. The company also arranged a system of heavy revenue collection from Bengal. Clive and the company men depleted the formerly very wealthy Bengal of its treasury so much that it led to a great deal of financial instability for the region. Clive later claimed in the

On June 23, 1757, Robert Clive and his troops defeated the forces of Siraj-ud-Daulah in the Battle of Plassey. This victory marked the beginning of British domination of India.

British courts that he used great restraint in his pillage. However, the financial loss caused by the British was so great that it was virtually irreparable and eventually led to a horrible famine in 1769–1770. The famine caused death by starvation of a third of Bengal's population. Jafar later felt shame for collaborating with the British. He at first thought it was for the betterment of Bengal. He had felt Siraj-ud-Daulah's recklessness and aggression to be dangerous. Then he realized the British were much worse with their greed and thirst for power over Bengal. He eventually rebelled, was removed and replaced, then, through an agreement, reinstated as nawab.

BRITISH REACTION TO EAST INDIA COMPANY AFFAIRS

The Battle of Plassey and the effects on the Indian people from the wars with the French were not favored by the British public. Employment with the East India Company had previously been looked upon as honorable, but now company men were viewed as barbarians for their conquests and plunders. Part of this change in view coincided with a change of cultural movement in England. England was now entrenched in the Romantic period, with the principle focus on the ethics and sensitivities of humanity. Many in England felt that the East India Company was exploiting the Indian people. They greatly objected to their actions. Plays were written to mock them, especially Clive after the Battle of Plassey. Many questioned why better diplomacy was not attempted. Those who were not concerned with the welfare of the people of India were convinced that the company would destroy itself through its military and territorial endeavors. Clive was brought to trial for his actions concerning the Battle of Plassey.

THE FINAL DEFEAT OF THE COMPAGNIE DES INDES

The Battle of Plassey—although not apparent at the time—was a milestone for the British, and it was followed by continuing military successes. During and after the break of fighting with the British, the French were not as lucky; instead the Compagnie was stricken with failure. The most impacting events upon their decline were the loss of their most important Indian ally and the continual defeats at the hands of the British.

In 1759, one of the company's staunchest supporters, the nizam of Hyderabad, was having difficulty in his position as ruler of one of the largest Mughal territories. Dupleix had installed him as ruler and through many military campaigns, the French second in command, Bussy, was able to retain the nizam in his throne against his competitors. However, when Dupleix returned to France, Bussy returned to Pondicherry, leaving troops at guard in the nearby Northern Circars. The nizam of Hyderabad granted the French the Northern Circars when he began his rule. However, the presence of the Compagnie troops was not enough to withstand the assaults by Clive, who sent a small detachment of company troops in a series of invasions against the Northern Circars from 1758 to 1759.

The purpose of the attacks was to oust the French from Madras, which they had attacked earlier in 1758. The British had retaken Madras, but the French were still stationed there, so the British attacked the Northern Circars to bring the fighting into French territory; the British feared another attack on Madras. The East India Company was astounded by its victory at the Northern Circars. It never expected to win with such a small number of troops. The Compagnie's loss of these battles made the nizam of Hyderabad distrust the powers of the French. He gave his alliance to the British. Furthermore, he granted the East India Company a section of the Northern Circars. The nizam had been one of the Compagnie's strongest allies. The British were thrilled to gain this new ally, who would form the perfect military shield for Madras.

After the surprise victory at the Northern Circars, the

East India Company sent more troops against the weakened Compagnie des Indes. Following these battles the British swept the French-controlled territory of Wandiwash. In 1761, the East India Company attacked and captured Pondicherry. The French, with the aid of a new, powerful ally, Haidar Ali, the ruler of Mysore, a Deccan principality, and his son Tippu Sultan, regained Pondicherry. However, even the regaining of their headquarters and support of a new power were not enough for the Compagnie des Indes. Their strength and finances continued to dwindle, while the East India Company continued to succeed.

In 1763, the Treaty of Paris brought an end to the Seven Years' War and also ended French and British hostilities in India. The treaty also brought an end to many of the activities of the Compagnie des Indes. The French were, for the most part, stripped of their power in India. They remained as a small presence at Pondicherry for their remaining trade holdings, but their influence and presence in India had otherwise ceased.

The East India Company had moved beyond being a company concerned with trade. In the time between receiving its *farman* and the defeat of the French, it had laid the groundwork for an empire within the already established British Empire. During this time it had received a great deal of territory as rewards in its many battles, and it boasted the influence of many political surrogates throughout India, some in the wealthiest territories of the country.

3

The British Conquering of India

The East India Company was able to attain vast territory and influence through involvement in Indian politics or king making, but some gains, as in Bengal, were effected through conquest. "The conquest of Bengal by the Company in Calcutta fuelled the ambitions of its Madras establishment in Mysore; Mysore's conquest opened the way to intervention in the Maratha territories; and the conquest of the Marathas brought the British up against the Sikhs." The wars for the most powerful territories in India were very destructive and full of atrocities, but victories became very lucrative for the British. The conquests became continuous, like a chain reaction.

THE MYSORE WARS

The kingdom of Mysore held a great disdain for the East India Company. There were several reasons for this, but the largest was the fear of British conquest. Mysore was previously an ally of the French; the Compagnie had given it military

After the conquest of Bengal, the British set their sights on conquering Mysore; thus began the period of the Mysore Wars. Pictured here is Tippu Sultan, sultan of Mysore from 1782 to 1799.

assistance and training in the use of European weaponry and in military tactics. After the battles at Pondicherry, the East India Company considered Mysore to be a major threat. Hyderabad was also concerned about Mysore. The nizam of Hyderabad had been dethroned by his brother, Nizam Ali. Both Nizam Ali and the company considered Mysore to be a problem and together they planned a common strategy. They decided to engage in battle with the anti-British Mysore. The First Mysore War began in 1767. The British and Nizam Ali thought they would easily defeat Mysore. They seriously underestimated the diplomacy and military strategy of Haidar Ali and strength and devotion of his son, Tippu Sultan.

Haidar Ali skillfully convinced Nizam Ali to defect from his alliance with the British and join forces with Mysore. The teenage Tippu Sultan led two successful raids upon Madras. "For the first time since Child's 'Mughal War' the British had been militarily checked by an Indian regime." Mysore had proved an equal opponent for the East India Company.

In 1769, the first Mysore War came to an end with the signing of a peace treaty. Under the conditions of the treaty, the British promised military aid if Mysore were to be attacked. The reputation of Mysore's strength and valor spread throughout India. Haidar Ali valued his treaty and was set to abide by its conditions.

The peace between Mysore and the East India Company, however, did not last for long. In the 1770s Mysore was repeatedly attacked by the Marthas. And despite their promises, the British never gave Mysore military aid. Mysore was nonetheless able to drive off the Marthas; impressed by Mysore's victory and alarmed by the broken promises of the British, other British allies and surrogates began to align themselves with Mysore.

In 1780 the angered Haidar Ali vowed vengeance for what he saw as acts of the greatest dishonor and untrust- worthiness and launched attacks upon the British in the Carnatic area near Madras. This was the perfect time to strike: British and French tensions had been renewed with the American War for Independence. This brought Haidar Ali the help of French troops. Another advantage was that the governor-general, Warren Hastings, was preoccupied with difficulties with the Marthas.

Haidar Ali launched the war on two different fronts; Ali led attacks around Madras, while Tippu Sultan struck Bombay. The Mysore army was once again very fierce and often victorious. The British made small gains that were later lost. In the Battle of Polilur in 1780 the British lost four thousand men, and only sixteen officers survived from the original eighty-six. Mysore, too, however, suffered great losses in this war. Haidar Ali died in 1782, and Tippu Sultan became the new ruler of Mysore.

Just as in the First Mysore War, the company was unable to make any gains in the Second Mysore War. In 1784 the Treaty of Mangalore ended the war, and victory was again with Mysore. The treaty had no real effect, however. It ended the battles but did nothing to alleviate the tensions.

Tippu Sultan, known by the British as the Tiger of Mysore, was angered by the British and felt that the treaty had been forced by the remaining French presence at Pondicherry. He therefore focused his attention on preparations for another war with the British. However, he now set his sights on gaining assistance directly from the center of the French government, at Versailles. He also sought the assistance of the international Muslim community. He created a twofold plan of diplomacy to better his war plans. In 1785, he sent a diplomatic envoy to Constantinople to lobby for the construction of a munitions factory there. In 1787, he sent emissaries to France to ask for financial and military assistance; however, France refused. Plagued by domestic problems, Louis XVI could not grant Tippu Sultan support. A year following Tippu Sultan's diplomatic mission, the Bastille would be stormed and the French Revolution would begin.

Not only did Tippu Sultan set forth in gaining alliances but he also followed his father's footsteps in westernizing his kingdom. But, whereas Haidar Ali had focused on bringing his military up to European standards, Tippu Sultan focused on the economy. He created his own trading company. He constructed many factories in Mysore—for silk processing, sugar production, and the manufacture of arms and ammunition.

Even without alliances Tippu Sultan was well supplied within his own means. Besides the British, only the Marthas held close to the amount of his artillery. He made his kingdom extremely wealthy, which made his regularly paid soldiers very loyal. After five years of planning, Tippu Sultan decided to launch an attack on the British in 1790.

The Third Mysore War began in 1790. The British were led by their governor-general, Charles Cornwallis. Cornwallis misjudged Tippu and Mysore when he prolonged the war in his pursuit of nothing less than absolute surrender. There was no way that Tippu Sultan would surrender. Cornwallis adopted a cautious approach. His misjudgment and overcaution were the result of his surrender at Yorktown, Virginia, which ended the American War for Independence with British defeat. The British could have ended the Third Mysore War swiftly with a low casualty rate, but Cornwallis's hesitancy prolonged the conflict.

Cornwallis forged an alliance with the Marthas and the nizam of Hyderabad. Cornwallis thought that Tippu Sultan would become fearful, but these alliances only made him angrier. Even though he was greatly outnumbered, Tippu Sultan and his forces held out for almost a year until they had to submit to British terms in 1792.

Governor-General Charles Cornwallis led the British to victory in the Third Mysore War. Although Tippu Sultan was defeated militarily, his kingdom quickly regained prosperity.

The British terms at the end of the Third Mysore War were very stringent. They required Tippu to make a large payment to the East India Company, hand over half his territories, and also his two young sons. When Tippu Sultan made his payment, after some debate, Cornwallis returned his sons. Cornwallis mocked Tippu Sultan by making claims that he had deprived him of all power. However, Tippu Sultan had made his kingdom so financially successful that Mysore immediately returned to prosperity. What Cornwallis and the company had taken was Tippu Sultan's power to challenge the British again.

The Fourth Mysore War began in 1799, soon after Richard Wellesley took his position as governor-general in India. Wellesley decided to invade Mysore owing to the fear of a possible attack by Napoleon. Napoleon had recently arrived in Egypt, and the company worried that he would come to India, where he was likely to attain victory. There had been rumors of Tippu Sultan meeting with Napoleon on the Indian Ocean and Mysore being supplied with troops. Wellesley documented the animosity between Mysore and Calcutta believed he was justified in launching an attack. Two other significant reasons were the glory of disposing of the Tiger of Mysore, who had boldly defeated the British in the past, and the fact of Mysore's great wealth.

Although called a war, the Fourth Mysore War involved a Mysore that was virtually defenseless. Its military power had vanished after the Third Mysore War. Wellesley sent more than forty thousand troops through the Mysore capital of Srirangapatna. The company troops, meeting little resistance, viciously pillaged the city and murdered more than nine thousand people. Tippu Sultan was found among the dead. He was both stabbed and shot several times and robbed of his belongings.

The troops swept through the rest of Mysore unchallenged. While storming the region, the company had the opportunity to also gain small neighboring territories on the coast of Karnataka. These territories, fearing Mysore's fate, willingly surrendered. The British awarded rule of the conquered territory to a political surrogate, an heir of the Wodeyar dynasty. He in turn bestowed Mysore upon the British.

THE REGULATING ACT OF 1773: PARLIAMENT ALTERS THE EAST INDIA COMPANY

In the 1770s, although the East India Company had achieved many conquests and large additions to its trade income through revenue collection, it was plagued by its many military ventures. It faced the possibility of financial ruin. It had been involved in constant military ventures since battles had begun with the French. Parliament was very concerned about this financial crisis. While Parliament was not supportive of the company's dangerous behavior and disorganized structure, its holdings in India were a very valuable asset. Britain did not want to lose its place in India; too much money was at stake.

In 1773 Parliament decided that the government needed to become directly involved in the affairs in India in order to more closely oversee Anglo-Indian affairs and exercise greater financial control. The government decided that, in place of loans, it would form a partnership with the company. Parliament passed a bill known as Lord North's India Bill, also known as the Regulating Act of 1773. The bill had a dual purpose: it would act as a watchdog over the company's actions and ensure financial stability. As part of the measure, it was determined that the best way to settle problems in India was through the rule of a Parliament-appointed governor-general.

WARREN HASTINGS

Warren Hastings was appointed the first governor-general of India in 1773. Hastings differed from Clive and many of the other East India Company men in the fact that he was a

Warren Hastings was appointed Britain's first governor-general in India in 1773. An enthusiastic student of Indian arts and philosophy, Hastings implemented a new approach to British interests in India.

wealthy man of high status. Hastings was interested in Indian culture. He was a great patron of Indian arts and held an enthusiasm for their philosophies. Hastings's first action as governor-general was to remove the false sovereignty set by Clive. Hastings removed power from the nawab of Bengal and discontinued tribute payments to the Mughal emperor. Hastings consolidated the governorships of

Bombay, Madras, and Calcutta, and ruled that all British sectors would be governed by the governor-general. Governing would thus no longer be fragmented.

Hastings took a different approach to military ventures than had Clive and his counterparts, whose focus eventually turned from financial gain to conquest. Hastings sought to form a glue for British interests in India. He did engage in what he saw as necessary military conflicts, such as with Mysore. He aided Oudh against the Rohillas of Afghanistan. He sought to bring an end to troubles with the Marthas. Hastings entered into treaties and alliances with powerful principalities. His main focus was diplomacy.

Hastings's various forms of diplomacy became very expensive, however, and it was necessary to regain the East India Company's large profit base. Financial improvement was one of the purposes of his assignment to India, but he was accumulating debt in his diplomatic campaigns. Hastings began to borrow from the wealthy Begums of Oudh and Raja Chait Singh of Benares. As debts from his military and diplomatic maneuvers continued to increase, however, it wasn't long before Hastings began to use extortion and the threat of force to secure loans.

The news of Hastings's unethical behavior in securing financial support eventually reached an angry and disappointed Parliament. Hastings resigned from his position of governor-general in 1784. He returned to face trial for his crimes, where he was impeached. His trials lasted for 10 years, and, at their conclusion, he faced bankruptcy.

THE MARTHAN WARS

During the 1700s the Marthas, who had been split into factions of different ruling families, united for the purpose of conquest. The strength of their military was able to absorb many smaller principalities. In the 1740s the Marthas ruled most of north and western India. They continued to achieve successful conquests through the 1750s. In the 1760s they reached the height of their power, when the highly respected Peshwa of Pune regained and stabilized Maharashtra, the Martha homeland. This was the crown jewel of Marthan conquests. Soon afterward Afghan troops launched attacks throughout the Marthan provinces. The Afghans were a strong military force, and the Marthas were defeated, with much damage inflicted in all the provinces, including Pune. Pune then sank into a dangerous succession crisis in 1771. Pune was the center of Marthan power and held the key to their beloved homeland.

The Marthan crisis gave the British the opportunity to attempt to quell the spirit of one of India's most powerful forces. The company's stockholders, however, were reluctant to endorse involvement in Marthan troubles. They wished to avoid the cost of unnecessary military expenditures. Hastings was ordered by Parliament and the stockholders to avoid involvement. Bombay did not, however, follow this order. Bombay was still bitter about the Marthan sea attacks around its borders. Moreover, Bombay was not ready to relinquish its governorship and follow the other bases under Hastings's consolidation of rule. Although the weakest of all the British bases, Bombay nonetheless engaged in 1775 in a war with the Marthans.

Although lacking capable forces, Bombay made an agreement in 1775 with the Marthas' leading contender, Raghunath Rao, to help enthrone him, in return for which he would grant the British the former Portuguese territories of Salsette Island and the port of Bassein. When Hastings and other company officials learned of this agreement, they were furious and ordered the immediate return of Bombay troops. Then Hastings formed a new diplomatic agreement with Raghunath Rao, removing the British from the Marthan conflict.

However, neither Bombay nor Rao followed Hastings's order. In 1778, Bombay's company troops fought on behalf of Raghunath Rao. Bombay's troops were completely defeated before they reached Pune. Immediately following the loss, Bombay signed the Convention of Wadgaon in 1779. This damaged the company's reputation. Hastings had sent troops to assist Bombay. The Marthas were able to hold the British back, but they were eventually defeated in 1781. The final treaty was signed in 1783. There were no territorial gains for either side from this war. Even though the company was victorious, no restrictions were placed upon the Marthas.

The Second Martha War was waged close to 25 years after the First Martha War. This war also stemmed from a succession crisis in Pune. Baji Rao II asked for British assistance, which would come with a heavy price. The British would have a strong influence on the government, such as a presence in the capital and troops within the territories. Richard Wellesley, the governor-general, saw the war as a way to expand British influence in India.

The Second Martha War began in 1803. The company was very quick to triumph this time and won other Marthan territories. The British gained a large amount of land in these battles. New alliances and territories brought problems with the nearby Sikhs. Their consumption of territory had cut into Sikh boundaries. A treaty was drawn to avoid conflict, which lasted successfully for 30 years.

The Second Martha War ended in 1804. It would have continued, but the company stockholders intervened. The stockholders had become irritated by the excessive spending of the ambitious Wellesley. He was recalled to England, and his departure brought the war to an end. The war did not dispose of the Marthas, but it impoverished their rulers and thus undermined their control. It left power mainly in the hands of the British through surrogate rulers and troops.

Wellesley's premature departure left the East India Company without direction in the Marthan situation. The British eventually withdrew from central India, overwhelmed by their own conquests. After their departure, chaos erupted throughout the region. The Martha leaders, impoverished after the war, began making raids in an attempt to restore their fortunes. The many soldiers of the Marthan princes, known as Pindaris, also turned to raiding. The British ignored the situation until the anarchy seemed beyond control.

In 1817 the company waged the Third Martha War. It was also known as the Martha-Pindari War. The British held the Pindaris responsible for much of the chaos in central India. The Martha leaders were coerced by threat of force to support the British. The third war was fought as a police effort.

During this war the British were in the process of forming a document that would revoke the powers given to the Peshwa in the previous war. The company felt that he had failed as a ruler and the Marthas would fare better under direct British rule. The Peshwa, Baji Rao II, felt deeply betrayed and attacked the company's resident in Pune and led his troops against British forces. His army was defeated, however, and he fled. His territories were seized and he was replaced with his son, Nana Sahib.

The Third Martha War ended in 1818. The conflict's end brought to a close the long-running Marthan rebellions and tirades, continuous since the reign of the Mughal emperor Aurangzeb. The only territory that remained completely under Marthan control was in their homeland of Maharashtra, in the small and peaceful territories of

Kolhapur and Satara. These territories were ruled by the direct descendants of Shivaji.

THE AFGHAN ENDEAVORS

In 1830 the company began to suffer from what can only be described as a "Russian phobia." At this time Lord William Bentinck, the governor-general, sent company men on a series of missions of exploration into Punjab and Afghanistan. The point of the missions was to determine if Russia had an opening into India. A great deal of India was now under British rule and alliance and it wanted to protect its assets. The company was concerned when it heard the Russian czar had an interest in India. The missions showed that a Russian foray into India would not be easy and was unlikely, however the company's paranoia was so great it was not completely assured. It was especially wary about Afghanistan's political policies. The company desired a presence in Afghanistan so it would have a blockade to protect India.

The opportunity came in 1833. The Sikhs were harboring the political fugitive Shah Shuja. Shah Shuja was the grandson of Ahmad Shah Abdali, ruler of Afghanistan. Shah Shuja gave the Sikh ruler the precious and very large Koh-i-noor diamond as a gift in exchange for his refuge. A large amount of Afghanistan's fortune was made from the plunder of many Indian regions. The Sikhs were angered by Ahmad Shah Abdali's actions. The British were interested in greater financial prospects, alleviating the Russian phobia, and in creating a protective land wall for India. The Sikhs and the East India Company combined forces and launched an attack upon Afghanistan, intending to enthrone Shah Shuja. They were, however, defeated in battle.

The East India Company's planned coup to replace the Afghan ruler Dost Muhammad with Shah Shuja ended in failure near Kabul, Afghanistan, during the First Afghan War.

The First Afghan War began in 1839 and was caused by failed diplomatic meetings between the British and the new Afghan leader, Dost Muhammad. Dost Muhammad decided to try to forge a deal with the company. He wanted the British to turn against the Sikhs, who had taken the territory of Peshawar, and aid the Afghans in regaining this territory. If the British helped him, Dost Muhammad agreed to resist any Russian attempted bribery or negotiations. Even though it meant the betrayal of an ally, the Russian phobia had so overtaken Lord Auckland that the company was considering the deal, until the summer of 1838. Lord Auckland received word that Dost Muhammad was consorting with the Russians and so refused any further negotiations with the Afghans. The company decided to undertake a coup in Afghanistan. The plan was to dispose of Dost Muhammad and replace him with Shah Shuja. The company gained the military support of the Sikhs. The British were very confident of winning. However, they were horribly defeated as they approached the capital of Kabul. The outcome was worst for the Hindu sepoy troops, who lost their status in their home regions: Hindu law dictated that, during the period of fighting, no one was allowed to leave India, so when the sepoys returned from Afghanistan, they were deemed outcasts. The loyalty to the company of many sepoys consequently fell as a result of the Afghan involvement.

The Second Afghan War closely followed the first and was more successful and thus boosted company pride. Nevertheless, although the evacuation of Kabul was achieved, no territory was gained. It seemed impossible for the company to attain its goals in Afghanistan, and it would therefore need to look for a territorial guard post elsewhere.

The company's answer came in 1843, when it conquered Sind, situated along the border of Afghanistan and India. Many company officials felt that seizure of this territory was unjust. The people of Sind were peaceful and had done nothing offensive to justify the attack of the British. The incursion was simply an attempt to create a land wall to protect India. The taking of Sind was very brutal, and the territory was ravaged by the company troops because the inhabitants did not willingly hand over their land.

THE SIKH WARS

In 1843, Ranjit Singh's successor was assassinated and a succession crisis broke out in Punjab. The British were tempted to become involved in the crisis for financial and political gain but held back. Instead, to prevent the fighting from spreading into their territory, they sent troops to guard the nearby are of Satlej. In 1845 more British troops were sent to the already large number posted there. Fearing the large contingent was intended to take advantage of the vulnerability caused by the succession crisis, the Sikhs resisted the British troops, thus beginning the First Sikh War.

The Sikhs won the first two battles in Ferozepur. But in 1846, in Sobraon, company troops routed the Sikh troops. The company then forced a treaty on the Sikhs. The treaty required annexations, established British residency, and stationed troops throughout Punjab; the Sikh army was reduced, and a political surrogate, Maharaja Dalip Singh, would be enthroned.

The Second Sikh War soon followed the first. The company's political activities and the imposition of Singh created grievances in the Sikh army about their loss of power, the British occupation, and unemployment.

In 1848 a Sikh garrison in Multan was attacked; two British soldiers were killed. Lord Dalhousie, the governor-general, decided to act with harsh vengeance to restore order. In fear of other mutinies, he dispatched a large number of troops throughout the entirety of Punjab. Instead of stopping rebellions, however, the violent attempts to quash tension only provoked more outbreaks.

Four months after the mutiny in Multan, Punjab stirred with chaos. The Sikhs requested help from Afghanistan. In order to avoid another Kabul, the company sent in more troops. The Second Sikh War had thus officially started. In the beginning of 1849, the Sikhs claimed the first battle. The British refused to publicly accept the obvious defeat. A month afterward the company ravaged the Sikhs in the Battle of Gujrat. This destroyed the Sikh force and led them to surrender.

On March 29, 1849, Maharaja Dalip Singh signed the Treaty of Lahore. The treaty surrendered Punjab to the British. Singh became a British pensioner, and British officials overtook Punjab. The extremely valuable Koh-i-noor diamond was given to Queen Victoria.

THE MUTINY OF 1857

The Mutiny of 1857 has been known by different names to the British and Indians. The incidents of 1857 have been referred to as the Sepoy Mutiny or the Indian Mutiny by the British, and as the Great Rebellion and later the First War of Independence by the Indians. More has been written of this incident than any other event in Anglo-Indian history.

The mutiny began as an uprising in the beginning of 1857 by company sepoy troops in Bengal. Although this was not the first sepoy mutiny, it was the largest and most effective. The others were quickly quelled, whereas this rebellion ran through different parts of India like an infectious disease. The seeds of the rebellion lay in the introduction of new rifles. The rifle was the final incident in the many mounting offenses by the company toward the cultural beliefs of the Indian sepoys. The new rifles required cartridges that were greased in pig and cow fat. The soldiers had to use their teeth to open the cartridges, which was completely repugnant in relation to the beliefs of both the Hindu and Muslim sepoys. Even when these

Viewing the East India Company's religious offenses as a devious attempt to convert them to Christianity, Indian sepoys staged an uprising during the Mutiny of 1857.

cartridges were withdrawn, the sepoys nonetheless held all official items as suspect, even the most basic items like flour and cooking oil. The sepoys no longer trusted the British. The sepoys saw the religious offenses as a sneaky way of the company to try to convert them to Christianity. The British were able to stop the dangerous rebellion that broke out in Bengal in February of 1857, but news of the incident spread rapidly.

The crushing of one rebellion only led to anarchy in another region. The next rebellion erupted in Meerut. The sepoys broke into and besieged the armory and attacked the European community. The mutineers then moved on to Delhi for the purpose of obtaining the cooperation of the Mughal emperor, the 82-year-old Bahadur Shah II. The emperor did not in fact have a choice on whether to support the rebels since he no longer had an army of his own and the British had vacated Delhi. The mutineers restored the old regalia of Mughal rule in Delhi, and Bahadur Shah II composed a ruling council for the mutiny. The main goal of the rebel sepoys was to rid India of the British. The Meerut rebellion inspired many military revolts, while the restoration of Mughal rule in Delhi led to many additional civilian uprisings. Everyone with a grievance against the British felt justified in rebelling. The enemy was not just the British, but anyone who could not prove that they were not involved with or benefited from the company.

The company did not, however, fight alone. The Sikhs and Gurkhas supported the British. The Sikhs had long held resentment against the Mughals, and they disliked the Bengal army. The British and their allies launched a two-month military strike against the Mughal emperor and the rebel sepoys. The company's eventual victory came with many casualties, and it vowed revenge: it killed the emperor's son and grandson and sent Bahadur Shah II into exile.

Other, smaller mutinies occurred in many different areas of India. Not all the sepoys participated, however. The sepoys in Madras and Bombay refused to disclaim their loyalty to the British. Most of southern India refused involvement, and the northwest was similarly uninterested.

When power had been taken from the Mughal emperor, the rebellion moved to the region of Oudh. The new leader of the mutiny was Nana Sahib, heir of the last Peshwa. Nana Sahib of Pune was very disgruntled with the British because they canceled his pension. In reaction to a mutiny in Kapurthala, the company launched a three-week siege, then moved on to settle the rebellions in Benares. Then news reached Nana Sahib that the British troops were en route to a mutineer base in Allahabad. He ordered the rescue of all women and children in the territory. It is possible that the plan was to use them as hostages. However, the sepoys panicked right before the British attack, which led to the killing of 200 women and children. The soldiers could not bring themselves to commit this action. Instead, men who worked in the bazaar, two of whom were butchers, performed the murders.

The British were stunned and murdered dozens of Indians in reprisal. Nana Sahib claimed to have no knowledge of the incident and fled. He knew the British needed a scapegoat and that he would be held responsible. Much like that of the Mughal emperor, Nana Sahib's role had been largely symbolic for both the sepoys and the British.

The most spectacular event for the British during the Mutiny of 1857 was the survival of Lucknow. Lucknow, the capital of Oudh, had fallen to mutineers toward the end of June 1857. A group of English women, children, and servants, and a small number of poorly armed British soldiers and loyal sepoys, sought shelter during the raids in the fortifications surrounding the British residency. The rebels made numerous attempts to take the residency. The people within the fortification withstood continual attacks until March 1858, when the British defeated the rebel sepoys.

This conflict in Lucknow ended the major rebellions.

Some very small mutinies continued in the countryside, but they did not present enough danger to require the attention of troops. After the Mutiny, sepoys were permitted to use whatever lubricant they wished for their rifle cartridges. By 1867 new rifles were in use that no longer required cartridge loading. New rules were set out for the army to guard against another rebellion. Indian troops would no longer receive artillery training. Sepoy recruitment was discontinued in areas where trouble had arisen during the Mutiny of 1857. However, recruitment was greatly increased in areas that had remained loyal to the Crown.

The East India Company now controlled most of India. The company, with help from home, and through influence, bargaining, annexation, king making, and military conquest, had managed to establish an entire empire. The Mutiny of 1857 demonstrated, however, the company's difficulties in ruling such a vast area, and so Parliament decided that it was finally time for India to evolve into an British Crown Colony.

4

The Westernization of India

When the Mutiny of 1857 was finally put down in 1858, Parliament decided it was time to deconstruct the East India Company. John Stuart Mill, the commissioner of correspondence at India House in London, pleaded on the behalf of the East India Company. However, the Mutiny of 1857 threw the company into complete and permanent disorganization. In the India Act of 1858, the rule of India was transferred from the East India Company to the British Crown. The transfer gave Britain authority to protect Indian states from internal and external threat and to exercise unlimited intervention in Indian affairs. A new form of government was put into place. Power in India was distributed among three presidents, in Bengal, Madras, and Bombay. The three presidents were under the jurisdiction of the secretary of state for India, a member of Parliament who was aided by an advisory Indian Council. In addition, India was split into two parts, British India, under direct rule of the Crown, and the Indian states ruled by the Indian princes. The country was also partitioned into provinces. This reorganization made for

With the transfer of Indian governance from the East India Company to the British Crown in 1858, the country became a Crown Colony. Queen Victoria became its empress in 1876.

easier rule and kept religious hostilities brewing, which in turn helped Britain sustain its power over India.

THE COLONIAL ECONOMY

When India became a Crown Colony it immediately gained a colonial economy. The implications of a colonial economy were that the entire nature of the economic system would be based on British needs. High taxation forced many peasants to sell themselves into work servitude for British land or factory owners, or into dangerous situations with moneylenders. Fluctuations in demand in the colonial economy sometimes led to mass unemployment. The one-way trade of the colonial economy favored the British. The colonial economy also dictated the taxation of natural resources, such as salt.

MODERNIZING INDIA

Now that India was a British colony, a first task was to modernize India. Modernization, in the context of 1858, involved transportation, communication, and industry. Roads were constructed and improved. Steamships were introduced into India for transport. The construction of a system of railways had begun in 1853, but efforts greatly expanded under colonization, particularly in the period 1870–1880. In 1869 the Suez Canal was completed, which greatly shortened the distance to India. Regarding communication, the introduction of the telegraph in 1870 made it possible to make direct contact between the British Isles and India. Industry expanded rapidly. Britain itself was in the midst of the Industrial Revolution. Many of Britain's leading industrialists were anxious to become involved in India. The products that had always been successful in the market were still selling very well. Many factories were established throughout India to mass-produce these products. The pay and conditions in the factories were abysmal.

QUEEN VICTORIA, EMPRESS OF INDIA

In 1876, the British government in India was restructured. Queen Victoria assumed the title of empress of India.

The three-president system was to be administered by a viceroy who would answer directly to Parliament. Many Indians were employed by the British government after these alterations. Queen Victoria pronounced that she would focus on the good of her Indian subjects. She and Parliament set forth to bring western ideas to India. They emphasized the importance of education, and established many schools in India. They also established universities. They brought many Indian scholars to study in England. Many of these students studied law and medicine.

Queen Victoria was a supporter of not only education in India but also women's rights and improvement of their living conditions. She was a great advocate of women's education in India, and worked to this end to establish additional schools for women. She also advocated many other rights for women, although sometimes, even as empress, she was not successful. She was concerned, too, with the general lack of any status of women in India, such as the right of widows to remarry and the appropriate age of marriage.

Queen Victoria became a cultural ambassador for India to Britain. She commissioned many public exhibitions in London to expose her people to all of the wonders of Indian culture. The exhibitions varied and included musical shows, dance, plays, art exhibits, visual displays of cultural scenes like the bazaars, and lecturers who taught the religions and philosophies of India. She wanted her subjects to learn of this mysterious land, the new jewel of the British Empire. Despite her efforts as cultural ambassador, Queen Victoria never traveled to India. She was very interested in India and had many photographs taken with props and Indian soldiers placed to make it appear that she was in India. The exhibits created a lot of excitement among the British. They were fascinated with

India, as was the rest of the western world. Indeed, the fascination was still evident almost 20 years later in the popularity of Rudyard Kipling's works, *The Jungle Book* (1894) and *The Second Jungle Book* (1895), which portray India as a place full of mythical events and magical creatures. It also established a picture of the British as being tamers of the wild. Kipling's works described very well how the British viewed India. He received the Nobel Prize for Literature for these books.

BRITISH INDIA

The British naturally had many cultural effects upon India, more so than the East India Company. That was because the government's purposes were very different. The company's aim was to secure economic profit; it had no wish to change India culturally. As a colony, however, it was now an appendage of Great Britain. The British felt it was their mission to civilize India. They assumed the Indians to be much more primitive than the Europeans and viewed the placement of British industry, government, medicine, culture, technologies, and lifestyles to be a great gift to the Indians, if not a blessing. Rudyard Kipling described the British intention in India with perfection when he wrote in his work *The Five Nations:*

> Take up the White Man's Burden—
> Send forth the best ye breed—
> Go bind your sons to exile
> To serve your captives' need;
> To wait in heavy harness,
> On fluttered folk and wild—
> Your new caught sullen peoples
> Half-devil and half-child

As part of the westernization of India, the British established the wide use of English games, such as cricket and polo. Pictured here is an Anglo-Indian polo team in Hyderabad, ca. 1880.

The British instituted not only British education but also English as the official language of India. They encouraged the Indians to establish journals, but they had to be published in English. Journals became very popular and India was home to many. They also encouraged the Indians to dress in European style, and eventually in fact, not doing so was highly discouraged and even forbidden in some places. Many Indians were fascinated with aspects of the British culture. For example, many enjoyed the games of golf, cricket, and tennis.

However, even while both groups enjoyed aspects of each other's culture, the Indians were treated with prejudice by the British. The British desperately wanted the Indians to be westernized but also desired a certain amount of segregation. The British considered themselves to be inherently superior to the Indians and refused them admittance by law into their homes, clubs, and certain restaurants. They were even discriminated against in branches of Britain's military.

SUPPRESSION OF SPEECH

Indians were encouraged to be educated but were permitted to use their knowledge only on certain levels. For example, there were restrictions on what Indian journalists could write: anything that seemed to call the British government's judgment into question was deemed unacceptable. There were, for example, articles concerning the devastating famines that began in 1866 and lasted until 1901. Indian journalists questioned why the British government had not done more to alleviate the famine conditions. The viceroy, Lord Lytton, passed the Vernacular Press Act, which forbade the spread of nationalist ideas, which was anything that disagreed with the British government. Another example is the withdrawal of the Ilbert Bill Act. This act allowed Indian lawyers to try British subjects. However, many British were angry by the passing of the bill and it was overturned.

THE INDIAN NATIONAL CONGRESS

It became increasingly necessary for Indians to have more of a voice in their government. Government employment was simply not enough. There needed to be a voice that represented the needs of the people of India.

There had been small meetings in the presidencies, but they were not effective. The Indian population needed a collective voice through representation. In 1885, a coalition of Indian lawyers and other professionals, under the assistance and the initiative of Allan Octavian Hume, founded the Indian National Congress to be such a voice. The Congress had direct contact with the viceroy. The members of Congress had learned the ways of British governing through the British school system and often had their concerns well received. The Indian National Congress was a gentlemanly organization. However, official political bodies like the Congress did not satisfy the concerns of all Indians. Not everyone felt their true interests were represented.

REBELLION IN BENGAL

Even though Britain had disbanded the East India Company and reorganized India through colonization and westernization, military strife did not end. The British colony of India was plagued with small rebellions aimed at freedom from oppression. Whereas these rebellions were small and short-lived, and of little political significance, a major rebellion—the largest since the Mutiny of 1857—took place in Bengal.

By 1905, rebellions in Bengal had grown very dangerous for the British. The rebels sought to free Bengal from British rule. They carried out a fierce campaign, assassinating British officials and dismantling British foundations and institutions. Bengal was a valuable holding, and the British did not want to lose this territory, nor did they want these incidents to inspire rebellion in other regions.

The solution to the Bengal rebellions came when the British decided to partition Bengal, separating western,

Hindu Bengal from the Muslim east. The British felt that it would be easier to impose their polices on a partitioned Bengal. However, this was not a plausible solution.

THE SWADESHI MOVEMENT

The Swadeshi Movement was the first large-scale non-violent protest in India. It was undertaken in reaction to the division of Bengal. The movement was comprised of nonviolent strikes, boycotts, and refusal of cooperation, which were carried out until their demands were met. The British gave in to the demands and removed the partition. After the compromises made as a result of the movement, the rebellions in Bengal ceased.

FORMATION OF THE MUSLIM LEAGUE

British government officials were concerned after the Bengal rebellions and the Swadeshi Movement that the Muslim community did not have enough involvement in government. They worried that if their voice was not heard it could also spark a rebellion.

There was Muslim representation in the Indian National Congress, but the majority of representatives were Hindu. Therefore, it was questionable whether the Congress truly represented the interests of the Muslim community. However, there was the belief that it was safer for the British to keep Hindus and Muslims divided. Since they had notoriously difficult relations throughout India's history, it was often easy to keep this division. The unification of these two groups could create a formidable power that might prove dangerous for the British government.

The British assisted the Muslim community in establishing the Muslim League in 1907. The Muslim community retained its representation in the Indian National Congress.

By 1907 British India had achieved its fourfold colonial government structure. There were two Indian assemblies, which represented the voice of the Indian people. There were three British presidents who each managed a section of the colony. The viceroy was the chief commander in India, who finalized all decisions and supervised the presidents. The viceroy also worked with and reported back to Parliament in England. Although the British government sought to correct the evils of the East India company and achieved some good in India, the British in India remained oppressors.

A Bridge to Freedom

The need soon came for the Indian representatives to go beyond just trying to establish a voice for the Indian public and also act as a defender of their rights. The Indian National Congress sometimes aligned itself with the Muslim League to gain concessions for Indians, but their joint calls were often unheard. They were dissatisfied with the ineffectiveness of their organizations upon government and felt themselves to be mostly symbolic. The British often used them as a tool to quell rebellions. The two representative bodies sought a way to gain betterment for their people and dreamed of independence from oppression, yet they did not have the tools at their disposal by which to seek such improvement and liberty. They also sought to preserve a cultural identity in the Indian people. The members of both groups became known as nationalists; they looked forward to an eventually free nation of India. The Congress and the Muslim League worked diligently toward these goals of betterment but were often unsuccessful, until one man's search for the truth built a bridge toward the betterment of standards and the eventual freedom for the peoples of India.

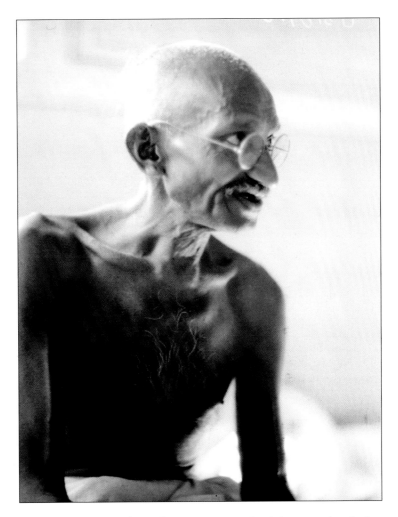

Mohandas Gandhi, the Mahatma, or Great Soul, became the single-most important leader in India's struggle for independence from British rule. The photo shows Gandhi soon after his release from British prison in Pune.

Mohandas Gandhi set forth on a lifetime quest to find the truth. His journey would lay the groundwork for release from Britain's shackles and eventual freedom for India. It is necessary to follow his life from the beginning in order to understand how one man in a single lifetime could, without drawing a weapon, defy such a powerful empire as Britain and lead his followers to freedom. He was able to accomplish such a feat by what he referred to as his search for the truth. His own journey prepared him for the quest for India's eventual freedom.

GANDHI'S EARLY YEARS

Mohandas Gandhi was born in Porbandar, Gurat, on October 2, 1869. Although his family was wealthy, it was part of the third-ranking Hindu caste, the merchant, or Vaishyas, caste. Gandhi was known as a happy child. He was earnest in his religious studies, which, following his mother's Hindu sect, involved learning from both Hindu works and the Qu'ran. He was a curious and adventurous child, often to be found exploring the bazaars near his home. Gandhi was also a very sensitive and caring child, which developed into the nurturing characteristics he was famed for in adulthood. As an example of his early gentleness, he was "one who would climb a mango tree in order, as he himself put it, to bandage the wounded fruit."

However, his teenage years brought forth great changes in Gandhi. At the age of 14, he was married to the 13-year-old Kasturbai. Gandhi was initially enthralled by married life, but this soon led to consuming feelings of jealousy. He refused to let Kasturbai leave the house to see her family or friends. She felt trapped by her duties as a wife, which led to many arguments. Mohandas became very depressed. He was searching for manhood, but his sadness led him toward rebellion. He experimented with a narcotic plant. Although married, Gandhi was still young and lived under the reign of his parents. He felt trapped. He tried suicide as an escape from his lack of freedom, and although his attempt failed, the rebellion continued.

Despite his family's protests, Gandhi bonded with a Muslim boy named Sheikh Mehtab, who promised to make a man of Gandhi. Sheikh Mehtab convinced Gandhi to join him in eating meat, smoking cigarettes, and making a visit to a brothel. He told Gandhi that if he took part in European pleasures, he would become strong like the English men. Gandhi rationalized the taking part in these actions that were so offensive to his culture as a way of trying to reform his friend.

Gandhi's rebellion ended in 1885 when his father became very ill. He stayed by his father's side throughout the ordeal, taking only one break to be with his wife. His father died in his absence. Shortly afterward, his own child died. Only 16 at this time, Gandhi blamed himself for the deaths and threw himself into the remaining two years of his studies.

GANDHI'S STUDIES IN LONDON

When Gandhi completed his studies in 1887, he decided to continue his schooling by studying law in England. This was forbidden by his family. "His mother resisted the idea, protesting that England would interfere with his Hindu principles and vegetarianism. A compromise, proposed by a family friend, was finally reached when, in the presence of his mother, Mohandas solemnly vowed not to touch wine, women or meat." This was not enough, however: his family members were not the only ones who objected to his European venture. The leaders of his caste forbade his departure from India, claiming it was an offense to his religion. Gandhi felt he needed to leave to further his studies and to escape his turmoil and misguided passions. He sailed for England, even against all of the objections. The caste religious leader excommunicated Gandhi and vowed to fine anyone who gave him assistance or saw him to his boat.

Gandhi was very enthusiastic about many aspects of western European culture. He was very fond of fashion and dressed very well. He was interested in learning and excelled beyond his law studies, learning French and the violin. He nonetheless kept the promises he made to his family in India. To support his practice of vegetarianism, he joined the Vegetarian Society in London. After he joined this organization, he decided to simplify his life—with the exception of his wardrobe—by living in self-imposed poverty. He had also kept his promise of abstinence from women.

Gandhi experienced a spiritual cleansing and awakening while in England. He studied the works of many different religions. He immersed himself in the Hindu Bhagavad Gita, which teaches one to abandon the material world for spiritual betterment. His enthusiasm for English culture led him toward a rediscovery of his own culture and what it meant to be Indian. Now that he was away from home, he was more in touch with his Hindu beliefs and Indian identity than while residing in his homeland. Gandhi's term of study in England laid the foundation for his search for the truth.

GANDHI TRAVELS TO SOUTH AFRICA

In 1891, Gandhi finished his studies and was made a member of the bar. He left England to practice law in Bombay. However, his shyness held him back as a lawyer, which caused him to fail in his cases. For example, in one incident he became so fearful and withdrawn that he was removed from the building by court officials. After such incidents, Gandhi realized that he needed to gain confidence and the art of persuasion to practice law. He also had to leave Bombay before he ruined his career. Gandhi decided to take a position in South Africa for a year.

To further his career as a lawyer, Gandhi left Bombay for South Africa, where the unjust treatment of immigrant Indian labor first aroused his political activism. Seated at center, Gandhi is pictured in front of his law office in Johannesburg.

Many Indians contracted themselves to work in South Africa for English and Boer employers for a five-year period. The workers made very poor wages and were treated badly. Their work conditions resembled those of slave labor. Many, however, sought such employment; some, for financial reasons, felt forced to seek it. Since there was large population of Indians in British-ruled South Africa, there was also a need for Indian lawyers.

Gandhi's new position allowed him to make his way to South Africa as a first-class train passenger. An Englishman on the train was angered when he saw Gandhi, an Indian, in first class. He demanded that Gandhi be removed from the train. Gandhi was thus forced to spend the night on a train platform. This moved Gandhi away from shyness and into his first political action.

When he finally reached his destination of Pretoria, he met with the local Indians to discuss the incident, as well as their own living conditions and lack of rights. He led protest meetings and eventually, through these actions, Indians gained the right to travel in first class as long as they were properly dressed. Gandhi was excited by his political involvement and decided to stay in South Africa beyond his one-year contract.

Gandhi and his family ended up staying in South Africa for almost 20 years. Gandhi felt that there was no truth in oppression, so his political movements sought to find and expose the truth in a betterment of living conditions. Only freedom held absolute truth. Gandhi organized many campaigns for the betterment of the conditions of Indian workers. He began petition campaigns, strikes, peaceful marches, and nonviolent protests. He stood up to the British leaders in South Africa on several occasions in appeals for the rights of Indian workers. He helped to repeal unfair taxes and restrictions upon the underpaid and overworked laborers. He led peaceful protests that overturned the many unjust laws. An example of these laws were the marriage laws that made all non-Christian marriages illegal and forbade Indian women to travel between provinces, and the Black Laws, which required all Indians to register, like cattle, through fingerprinting. He and Kasturbai, who stood by him in all in his endeavors, were imprisoned a few times for their political involvement. Gandhi often implored the Indian National Congress to enact such improvements in India, but he was continually unsuccessful.

Gandhi also undertook great spiritual examination and study while in South Africa, eventually shaped the face of the Indian movements in South Africa and in his homeland of India. Gandhi underwent a spiritual cleansing while in South Africa. He sought to simplify his life and abandoned the status of his Hindu caste by doing menial labor that was considered to be work suitable only for untouchables. He began to perform such scandalous acts as cutting his own hair, cleaning the toilet, washing his own clothes, and housecleaning. He embraced the philosophies of the Bhagavad Gita and abandoned all material goods. He ate very simple meals, just enough to sustain himself, and abandoned his beloved European attire for the traditionally Indian handwoven white robes. His wife, Kasturbai, although at first very reluctant, eventually followed suit in this lifestyle, and together they formed an ashram, a place of seclusion for prayer and spiritual practice.

Gandhi also studied a great deal and wrote while in South Africa. He gained much of his political ideology from this time of spiritual expansion. For example, during one of his terms of imprisonment, he studied Henry David Thoreau's work, *Civil Disobedience,* which outlined a blueprint for making a statement or attaining one's rights through civil disobedience. The philosophy of civil disobedience, as examined in Thoreau's book, was a way of promoting and attaining a political belief or movement by enacting a peaceful resistance. For example, Thoreau objected to the Mexican War, and used civil disobedience by refusing to pay his taxes. Gandhi was entranced by Thoreau's work and the philosophy of civil disobedience and sought to apply the practice to his own struggles and search for the truth. In his developing beliefs, he combined his understanding of truth and his desire for political action in a concept he called "satyagraha." He described satyagraha in the following terms: "Satyagraha is pure soul-force. Truth is the very substance of the soul." Blending this concept with Thoreau's philosophies, he believed that "soul-force" would enable the action of civil disobedience. "We can . . . free ourselves of the unjust rule of the Government by defying the unjust rule and accepting the punishments that go with it."

GANDHI'S RELATIONS WITH THE BRITISH

Although the British, as the oppressor, were the enemy in his search for the truth, Gandhi always dealt with them in a gentlemanly manner. He even aided the British by starting the Indian Ambulance Corps and received medals for his service as a stretcher bearer during wartime. Before taking action, Gandhi always sought negotiation first, and if that was not possible, he gave the leading British official prior notice of his intended action and its cause. He also took care to never insult his enemy. In one such case, while leading workers in protest, he learned that a British railway workers' strike was forming, and so he ceased his own act of protest. He also always demanded the strictest punishment when put on trial. He dealt with the British with great civility and empathy in their times of trouble in South Africa, and continued this behavior in his political involvement in India.

GANDHI RETURNS TO INDIA

When Gandhi returned to India in 1914, he was greeted enthusiastically by the top Indian leaders, Bal Gangadhar Tilak and Gopal Krishna Gokhale. They were very excited by his accomplishments for the betterment of Indian conditions in South Africa. They were now anxious to learn about his ideas for India. It was necessary for Gandhi to become reacquainted with his homeland first, however. He had resided in South Africa for more than 20 years. His first year back, he remained politically inactive and simply traveled throughout India. During his travels, he experienced the oppression and poverty of his homeland. At this time the poet Rabindranath Tagore gave Gandhi the title Mahatma, which means great soul, for his work and gentle manner. Gandhi wrote at this time *Hind Swaraj,* a work opposing British rule in India. He also started an ashram near Ahmadabad. It was here that Gandhi began his efforts to free and unite the Hindu caste system. He angered and surprised many Hindus when he admitted into the ashram a family of untouchables. He lost grants for this action, but kept to his convictions.

THE BEGINNING OF GANDHI'S POLITICAL CAREER IN INDIA

Gandhi began his career in India in 1916 when he started attending sessions with the Indian National Congress. Not long after being involved with the Congress, Gandhi was approached by peasant indigo growers from Bihar. The farmers of Bihar were being exploited by their British landlords. In addition to rent, they were forced to devote three-twentieths of their land to the growth of indigo and give all of the profits to the British landlords. The farmers asked Gandhi to stop this exploitation. Gandhi researched the situation and

After residing in South Africa for more than 20 years, Gandhi and his wife, Kasturbai, returned to India in 1915. It was shortly after his return to India that Gandhi earned the title Mahatma, or Great Soul.

approached the court with the matter, accompanied by other Indian lawyers and thousands of farmers. Gandhi proposed that the British landlords return 50 percent of the indigo revenue to the destitute Bihar farmers. The British agreed to

Kasturbai Gandhi: India's Silent Heroine

Kasturbai Gandhi, wife of the famous Mahatma, was a courageous woman who played an important part in the Indian independence movement. She has not received the acknowledgment she deserves. Besides the fact she was Gandhi's wife, little is generally known about her. More than just the assisting wife of Mohandas Gandhi, she was a political and spiritual leader in her own right.

Kasturbai, like her husband, was deeply spiritual. At first she strongly objected to her husband's abandonment of the rules of the Hindu caste system and his determination to, for example, perform menial labor as part of his new spiritual lifestyle. More than an aversion to cleaning toilets, Kasturbai's concern was with abandoning important aspects of Hinduism, which, according to Hindu teaching, would result in excommunication and serious spiritual consequences. Kasturbai did not want harm to fall upon their four sons, Harilal, Manilal, Ramdas, and Devadas, as a result of their father's religious experiments and ideals. Gandhi himself often described her as free spirited and strong willed. He spoke of how Kasturbai's independence created differences in the earliest years of their marriage: "She made it a point to go out whenever and wherever she liked. More restraint on my part resulted in more liberty being taken by her, and in my getting more and more cross." Despite her earlier objections, Kasturbai listened to Gandhi's teachings on his new spiritual understandings. Whereas Gandhi had the ability to support his faith in the continuous study of books, Kasturbai was illiterate and had only her heart to turn to. She searched her soul and eventually decided to join her husband in his simplified spiritual life. With the responsibility of caring for her husband and children, however, she was not as free as Gandhi to make a quick transition. Kasturbai was also a prominent political figure. She believed strongly in the need to improve living conditions for Indians and in the cause of Indian independence. She was an active participant in her husband's political career. She was always by Gandhi's side. In South Africa, to protest the marriage laws, she led a group of women in peaceful protest. She was imprisoned in a hard-labor camp for this infraction. She was often imprisoned in India alongside her husband.

In order to be more effective in the political arena, she worked at learning to read and write. She often sent simple letters to many regional leaders seeking support for the cause. Kasturbai was a very powerful speaker and often spoke in support of women's rights in India and to encourage women to join the nationalist cause. Her speeches were very successful, and she inspired many throughout India. She also took over the leadership of many peaceful demonstrations after her husband had been either imprisoned or detained by other matters. Kasturbai was, in the end, a martyr for the cause of India's independence: after giving a public speech, she was arrested and, on February 22, 1944, died in prison in her husband's arms.

only 25 percent. Although not a complete financial success, the compromise was nonetheless a great victory; it was a blow to the power of the British landlords.

The "removal of the stain of indigo," as it became known, led Gandhi to become the champion of a movement to aid textile workers. The workers in the British textile factories received barely livable wages and worked long, strenuous hours. They sought Gandhi's help, who advised them to strike until their demands were met. The workers followed Gandhi's advice and continued to strike for many days, but it was to no avail. Gandhi struggled with ideas on how to improve the workers' resistance. He decided to take it upon himself, and he fasted for three days until the workers' demands were met.

WORLD WAR I

Since Gandhi's return to India, Britain had been involved in World War I, which is why he attacked only private industry. He sought to aid the British in their dangerous struggles after hearing of the horrors of this war. In 1918 he launched a campaign to recruit Indians to aid the British in their plight. It is possible that he felt Indian involvement would later be a valuable bargaining tool. What prevailed, however, was Gandhi's empathy for his oppressor. Gandhi worked very hard on this recruitment, severely compromising his health, almost to the point of death. Eventually, his poor health forced him to stop, but not before he was successful in recruiting many men. However, the Indians who enlisted before and after Gandhi's campaigns were still treated with great prejudice.

World War I ended successfully for the British, but Indian assistance did not make a difference in matters in India. The British were concerned with rumors of rebellion. In 1919 they set forth a whole new set of restrictions through the Rowlatt Acts, which removed Indian entitlement to a trial. In response, Gandhi proposed a *hartal*. A *hartal* is a silent protest in which the demonstrators take part in prayer and all social activity ceases. The Indian nationalist leaders agreed, and Gandhi gave the viceroy notice of the *hartal* that would bring silence to Delhi. On March 30, 1919, the *hartal* occurred and the entirety of Delhi shut down.

The British were angered by the power of the peaceful movement in Delhi: Delhi had been completely immobilized. The British decided to take action. On April 13, 1919, during a peaceful demonstration of some twenty thousand people in Amritsar, the British army, without warning, repeatedly fired into the crowd. "General Reginald Dyer . . . was in charge of the operation, which killed more than three hundred people and wounded almost a thousand others. He had ordered his men to fire into the thickest part of the crowd." Gandhi was horrified by these events and canceled the resistance movement.

THE NONCOOPERATION MOVEMENT

The noncooperation movement began as a reaction to the British actions at Amritsar. Hindus and Muslims agreed to full unification at the Muslim Conference of November 24, 1919. The unity of the two groups was seen as the perfect launching pad for Gandhi's plan of noncooperation. The idea behind noncooperation was to discard all things British. To begin the movement, the Indian National Congress invented new slogans, but even more important, a new flag. The flag portrayed the *charkha,* the traditional spinning wheel. Gandhi returned his medals and led people in public rallies to burn their European clothing. Gandhi and other members of the Congress encouraged people to wear traditional Indian clothing made from cloth spun on the *charkha*. Students abandoned European learning institutions in favor of Indian centers of learning. Gandhi and other lawyers renounced their European occupations. Gandhi now referred to himself as a farmer and weaver. The noncooperation movement spread far and was embraced throughout India.

The British were distraught over the actions of noncooperation. They needed to regain order. In November 1921, Edward, the Prince of Wales, traveled to India with the hope of settling the tensions. However, the Indian National Congress refused to meet with Prince Edward. His visit led to a number of riots. By December the British had imprisoned close to twenty thousand Indians. After the Prince's disastrous visit, Rufus Daniel Isaacs, first marquess of Reading, was installed as viceroy to calm the tensions. The new viceroy sought negotiations with Gandhi, but the two could not come to a compromise.

Since the British refused to agree to any of the conditions of the Indian nationalists, the next step in noncooperation was to launch a civil disobedience movement in Bardoli. Gandhi informed the viceroy of the plan. Unfortunately for the plan to effect a peaceful movement, it went astray: when the police approached the demonstrators, their anger for their oppressors overcame them. In response to police arrests and brutality, they attacked the officers and burned them alive.

Gandhi was horrified by this display of violence; when he was arrested, he took responsibility and demanded the highest penalty. The viceroy did not want Gandhi imprisoned because he did not hold him at fault for the violence, but he nevertheless conceded to his demands and Gandhi was given a prison term of six years. The imprisonment lasted for only two years, however, because Gandhi was

As the noncooperation movement gained strength in India and tensions mounted between Britain and India, Britain decided to send Prince Edward to the colony in the hope of easing hostilities. His visit failed and violence only increased. Here the prince inspects troops in Bombay.

released for appendicitis. During Gandhi's imprisonment, the noncooperation movement ceased as tensions between Hindus and Muslims resurfaced.

HINDUS AND MUSLIMS

The Hindu and Muslim communities had a long history of turmoil but had conceded to work together in the campaign of Indian nationalism. It seemed as if Gandhi had been the glue that held them together. Before Gandhi's emergence into Indian politics, their struggles had been disabled by lack of agreement between the two groups. Although Hindu, Gandhi had knowledge of the Qu'ran and was unprejudiced, so he was able to maintain very good friendships with many Muslim leaders. Upon his release from prison, Gandhi's first priority was the reunification of the Hindu and Muslim nationalists. He was very disappointed when he found that the situation had grown well beyond the point of discussion. He feared a violent outbreak between the two groups. He decided on a fast to bring the two communities together. There would be no chance for the Indian nationalist cause to attain either an improvement of living conditions or the eventual goal of independence if the two groups were not together. The fast lasted 21 days. The leaders of both communities reconciled and together held a vigil at his bedside. After breaking the fast, Gandhi traveled throughout India to gain support for the nationalist movement.

GANDHI IS NOMINATED PRESIDENT OF THE INDIAN NATIONAL CONGRESS

Near the end of 1925, after the reuniting of the Hindu and Muslim nationalists and Gandhi's latest campaign through India for the promotion of Indian nationalism, the Indian National Congress elected Gandhi president. However, he felt compelled to embark upon his own personal yearlong spiritual journey and so declined the nomination. He handed the presidency over to the poetess Sarojini Naidu, who followed Gandhi's example in organizing peaceful civil disobedience movements, but on a much smaller level. In Gandhi's absence, other nationalists pursued their political interests in more violent movements.

THE BRITISH COMMISSION

When Gandhi made his political reemergence in 1927, he and the other nationalists were met with a new and different problem than they had previously encountered in their struggles.

The viceroy, Edward Frederick Lindley Wood, Baron Irwin, called the Indian National Congress and the Muslim League to a conference in which he informed them that a commission from England was being sent to compile a report on India and, further, that there would be absolutely no Indian involvement in the matter. The Indian nationalists were enraged that the people of India had been dismissed in such a manner, as if, in the eyes of the British, they were nonexistent or less than human. They believed the Indian people should always have input in matters pertaining to their country.

Gandhi immediately proposed plans for a peaceful protest. However, many of the new, younger members of the movement were not satisfied with Gandhi's methods and thought more could be done through violent rebellions. The two groups could not come to an agreement. Over the next few years, Gandhi and his followers engaged in peaceful protests, *hartals*, acts of civil disobedience, and marches. These movements were met with imprisonment and beatings, but they were more successful than the violent rebellions, which were met with refusal to negotiate, vengeance, and death. The peaceful resistance of Gandhi and his followers brought gains, even if only at times modest ones, whereas the violent actions of the other camp sometimes hurt the movement. As a result, many of the nationalists began to favor Gandhi's ideas of peaceful resistance. This did not, however, end the violent campaigns for freedom.

6

The Road to Independence

The Indian National Congress and the Muslim League decided it was now time to look beyond the struggle for rights and equality and eventual independence. They decided it was time for nothing short of complete independence from imperial Britain. In December 1929, the Indian National Congress gave Britain a year's notice of India's declaration of independence. Following this proclamation, campaigns of violence ran rampant throughout India, such as the bombing of the British legislative hall in Delhi. Britain felt that a way to control the chaos was to change India's status from a colony to that of a dominion. A conference was planned to discuss the future of India. However, radicals bombed the viceroy's train and the conference was canceled. On January 26, 1930, under the leadership of president Jawaharlal Nehru, the Indian National Congress declared India's independence from Britain. They flew the tricolored flag bearing the *charkha*. Nehru, whom Gandhi affectionately referred to as his spiritual son, called for all of India to act with civil disobedience and not submit to Britain's rule. Britain's response was to try

In one of the most symbolic acts of Indian defiance against British tyranny, supporters of Gandhi and his nationalist cause break British salt laws by filling containers with seawater near Bombay on May 7, 1930.

to persuade the nationalist leaders to attend the First Round Table Conference in England in 1930, which the Congress boycotted.

THE SALT MARCH

Gandhi desired to encourage the Indian public to stand behind the movement for independence and engage in actions of civil disobedience. He decided that he needed to do something on a large scale that would affect the entire population. His answer was the attack on the salt laws. The British had enacted laws controlling salt, a resource needed in every household and one that was easily accessible naturally on the shores of India. It was illegal for Indians to obtain salt on their own or to sell it; rather, they needed to purchase it from the British and pay the heavy taxes levied on it. Gandhi sent a letter to the viceroy, Lord Irwin, on the matter of the unfairness of the salt laws, and he outlined his plan of action if the government did not comply to correcting this injustice. Gandhi stated in his letter: "I shall proceed with such co-workers of the Ashram as I can take, to disregard the provisions of the salt laws. I regard this tax to be the most iniquitous of all from the poor man's standpoint. As the independence movement is essentially for the poorest in the land the beginning will be made with this evil." The viceroy dismissed the matter and did not see its relevance in the current state of affairs.

On March 12, 1930, Gandhi set out from his ashram in Sabarmati en route to Dandi. He embarked with close to 80 followers and stopped in each town along the way to talk about injustices in India and to encourage Indians to resist the salt laws. Many left their work and homes and followed him to Dandi. The journey was a distance of 375 km and took 26 days to complete. When he reached Dandi, he spent the night consumed in prayer. In the morning he led his followers to the water and committed the illegal action of scooping up a handful of salt. The thousands that followed also began to scoop up salt with their hands. After this, salt was illegally sold in villages throughout India, and almost the entirety of India ignored the salt laws, and many were further inspired to stop paying all of their taxes and not purchase European goods. Sixty thousand arrests were made as a result of the salt march and illegal trade in salt. Gandhi was arrested a month after the incident.

The effects of the salt march did not end with Gandhi's arrest. He arranged for his son, Manilal, and Sarojini Naidu, the former president of the Indian National Congress, to lead a peaceful march against the Dharasana Salt Works. On May 21, 1930, close to three thousand anti-salt law protesters approached the salt-processing factory. They were continually attacked by police, but they did not give up, resist, or resort to violence. This incident received global attention.

KHAN ABDUL GHAFAR, THE FRONTIER GANDHI

Gandhi and Nehru were not the only nationalist leaders organizing peaceful resistance movements. Khan Abdul Ghafar, a close friend of Gandhi, was known as the frontier Gandhi because he took the movement to the less-accessible and often forgotten areas of northwest India. He organized civil disobedience movements in this region. The people of this area felt oppressed and were very devoted to the cause. In one year close to 90,000 people were imprisoned in the area. The most famous moment in Khan Abdul's campaigns was in 1932, when the 13-year-old Rani Gaidilita waved the Indian nationalist flag in sight of British soldiers during a peaceful demonstration, and she was therefore sentenced to a lifetime imprisonment. She became an inspiration for the movement throughout the entirety of India, as well as a symbol of freedom itself. She was not released until India gained its independence in 1947.

GANDHI'S DIPLOMATIC MISSION TO ENGLAND

The Indian National Congress decided to accept Britain's second invitation to a conference. The British agreed to release all of the movement's imprisoned leaders if they would agree to attend the conference and temporarily halt the civil disobedience movement. Most of the leaders were

The Indian National Congress sent Gandhi to London in September 1931 to attend the Second Round Table Conference. During his stay, Gandhi dressed in traditional Indian clothing and insisted on lodging in London's poorest quarters.

imprisoned, so Nehru and the Congress agreed. They sent Gandhi to London in September 1931 to attend the Second Round Table Conference.

Gandhi was well received in London and adored by the British press and public. He stayed in London from September 12 to December 5, 1931. Gandhi refused offers to stay in the finest hotels and instead took residence in the poorest quarters in London. He dressed in his normal traditional Indian robes, even when dining at Buckingham Palace. Curious about industry linked to India, he visited textile factories. He also received high accolades from his speaking engagement at Oxford University.

The focus of Gandhi's mission to the conference was to gain an independent India and equality with Britain. Britain's purpose was to end the civil disobedience movements.

The British had no intention of granting independence but were willing to concede to more direct representation. This proved disastrous, because every religious group in India insisted on its own representation. No agreements were made at the conference. After traveling throughout Europe, Gandhi returned to India.

A DANGEROUS IMPRISONMENT

When Gandhi returned from Europe, he found that most of the nationalist leaders and more than sixty thousand supporters had been imprisoned, Nehru and the Muslim leader, Tasadduq Cherwani, among them. The new viceroy, Lord Freeman Willingdon, had imposed many new restrictions in Gandhi's absence. It was now forbidden to hold political assemblies or associations of any kind, demonstrations, boycotts, rallies, or anything else of an anti-British nature. Lord Willingdon refused to meet with Gandhi under any terms. Gandhi was imprisoned a month following his return.

While in prison in 1932, the nationalist leaders learned of a Third Round Table Conference, which the nationalists did not attend because most of their leadership was imprisoned. The British were in the formative stages of drafting a constitution for India and a restructuring of government in which they intended to give every religious group its own representative on a council. The British were also creating a representative position for the untouchables. Gandhi was enraged by this action, particularly by the continued separation and discrimination of the untouchables. The untouchables were not a separate group, they were part of the Hindu caste system. Gandhi immediately drafted a letter to the secretary of state for India, Sir Samuel Hoare. Gandhi wrote that if the government did not change its stance he would fast to death. He was ignored, and the government decided on separate elections for the untouchables on August 17, 1932. Gandhi began his fast on September 20, 1932.

The remaining Hindu leaders who were not imprisoned sought a meeting with the leader of the untouchables, Dr. Bhimrao Ramji Ambedkar. He was a lawyer and viewed British or Muslim rule to be preferable to Hindu governance. He initially ignored Gandhi's fast. After three days, however, he agreed to meet with Gandhi. He visited Gandhi on September 23; Gandhi was already near death and could barely speak. He convinced Ambedkar of his devotion to the cause of equality for the untouchables. He negotiated the number of representatives for the untouchables. The Hindus and untouchables signed the Yervada Pact, and a confirmation was received from England.

All of India followed the state of Gandhi's health throughout his fast. There were constant news updates on the radio about his pulse and blood pressure. The beginning of his fast brought forth a new existence for the untouchables. They were allowed in temples and had contact with members of all castes. The Yervada jail, where Gandhi was imprisoned, was flooded with signed letters promising better treatment of the untouchables.

After the fast, Gandhi was tired and felt physically strained. When he was released from prison in 1932, he participated in a few small civil disobedience demonstrations. In 1934 he felt that independence was definite; he resigned his position in the Congress. He trusted his beloved Nehru to continue seeking the truth and went into political retirement. He did not, however, remain inactive: he focused on speaking to

Although the Indian National Congress favored Indian participation in World War II in exchange for independence, Gandhi was firmly opposed to joining Britain's fight. Here Gandhi is shown arriving in Delhi in 1939 to discuss the issue of Indian independence with the British viceroy.

people on becoming in tune with their Indian identity. He also entertained visitors who sought to speak with him after hearing of his work from around the world.

THE GOVERNMENT OF INDIA ACT

In 1935, Parliament proposed an idea to establish a solid Indian role in government. Earlier attempts at government had been mostly symbolic, but this time Parliament sought to find a new system of government based on provincial autonomy. This meant there would be elections for representatives from each province in India. There would also be a section of government entitled the Congress of Ministry. The job of the Congress of Ministry would be to seek amnesty for political prisoners and protect the civil liberties of the people. However, since this was a limited democracy within a sovereignty, the Congress of Ministry was unlikely to be effective. Parliament felt that this gesture would satisfy the nationalists' desires to have their own government, albeit one constrained within a sovereignty, while preserving Britain's profitable place in India. Parliament passed the Government of India Act in 1935 and thus allowed for this federation.

The elections for representation were held in July 1937. The Indian National Congress Party was very successful in the elections, winning the votes in seven of the provinces. The Muslim League did not fare as well, gaining only a quarter of the representation in the seats set aside for the Muslim population. Mohammad Ali Jinnah, who was the permanent leader of the Muslim League, was very dissatisfied and feared that Muslim interests were endangered under the Hindu majority. Jinnah began to seek a form of separation for the Muslims from the Hindus. The new government structure did not disband the nationalist Indian National Congress or the Muslim League.

WORLD WAR II

In 1939 Britain became involved in World War II. Regarding the war effort, the viceroy, Victor Alexander John Hope, involved India unilaterally in terms of industry and troops. All factories were immediately converted toward war manufacturing. The viceroy also expected Indians to enlist to fight for Britain. The Indian National Congress was very angry by this assumption. The viceroy declared this involvement without consulting any faction of the Indian section of government, nor any sector of the nationalist movement, which still retained the position as the voice of the Indian public. The Congress informed the viceroy that if Britain desired aid from India, it must allow India to determine the nature of that aid. India would not be forced to fight for Britain. As far as industry was concerned, being mainly under British ownership, it was, with little incident, channeled toward the war effort.

The emergence of World War II brought Gandhi back into the realm of Indian politics. The majority of the Indian National Congress were strongly antifascist and appalled by the actions of Hitler. Gandhi pleaded with the Congress not to become involved in World War II. He was greatly disturbed by Hitler, but felt it was best for India to remain unengaged in this conflict. Many in Congress insulted him for his attitude, especially in the light of his earlier efforts during World War I. He explained that he no longer found truth in war or actions of violence. For the first time, the Indian National Congress, which he was no longer a member of, did not listen to Gandhi. They had disagreed before, but this time they refused to take his ideas into consideration. On September 14, 1939, the Indian National Congress offered Britain military aid if it agreed to grant India its independence.

Winston Churchill, the British prime minister, absolutely refused to make a deal with the Indian National Congress for independence on any terms. He was infuriated by India's nationalist movement and had often made public statements insulting Gandhi and his followers. Churchill began his service to Britain as a soldier in India during his youth. He adored British India and did not want to see it fall, especially during his term as prime minister. Churchill stated of India: "I have not become the king's first minister in order to preside at the liquidation of the British Empire." He was also determined to make sure that India did not gain any major political concessions during this time of Britain's

Winston Churchill, the British prime minister, was staunchly opposed to Indian independence. In response to Gandhi and the drive for independence, Churchill stated: "I have not become the king's first minister in order to preside at the liquidation of the British Empire."

vulnerability. He instructed the viceroy that, in exchange for military service, the Congress would gain representation on the war advisory board.

The Congress was not happy with the terms and looked to Gandhi for a solution. He complied by directing that a group of representatives from Congress be sent throughout India to encourage the people to join a noncooperation movement against the war effort. He called for some actions of peaceful demonstration, but kept the movement limited. Gandhi limited the movement out of respect for his enemy; he did not want to distress them in their time of war.

In the spring of 1941, the war was moving close to the borders of India. Many feared that the Japanese and Germans would combine forces in India. Many other regions throughout Asia had been invaded. Japan had even threatened an attack upon India. President Roosevelt of the United States continually pressured Churchill to compromise with the Indian nationalists. The conquering of India would be a huge devastation to the Allies. The Indians were also in fear after all of the horrible stories they had heard about Hitler. Churchill sent Richard Stafford Cripps with an offer to the Congress that India would become a dominion with its own assembly after the war. There was also the condition that one-third of the assembly would be composed of maharajahs loyal to the Crown. The Congress was not pleased with this arrangement and lacked complete trust in the British bargain. However, with the fear of invasion they had to combat not only the British but also the youth of India, who were strongly antifascist and desperate to enlist in the war effort.

QUIT INDIA

The nationalists needed to spring quickly into action before many men decided to enlist and the nationalists would be forced to abide by the British terms. On April 13, 1942, Gandhi proposes the Quit India Movement; it was to entail a revolution of civil disobedience and cries for freedom. In this nonviolent initiative, Gandhi stressed that

Indians should do their utmost to seek freedom or die trying. He challenged them to no longer be slaves of oppression and win freedom by putting their lives on the line in nonviolent resistance. For three weeks he negotiated with the public and the viceroy. However, on the day the movement was to begin, he and all of the leaders of the Indian National Congress were imprisoned. The Indian National Congress was deemed as being illegal. The only nationalist leader who had not been imprisoned was Mohammad Ali Jinnah, leader of the Muslim League. Churchill had been anxiously awaiting an opportunity to capture Gandhi and disband the Congress.

The imprisonment of its leaders did not stop the movement. However, it was not a peaceful resistance. The public was enraged, protesters shouted out: British Quit India! The movement turned very violent, the violence sweeping through India. Several British citizens and institutions were attacked. There were revolts, acts of terrorism, mass murders, and arsons.

The viceroy, Linlithgow, held Gandhi personally responsible for the violence. Gandhi denied this accusation and constructed a letter in reply. This was to no avail. Gandhi then proceeded with a fast for three weeks to amend this injustice and all of India rallied behind him. Viceroy Linlithgow refused to concede to what he considered to be political blackmail and ignored the fast. Gandhi was soon struck with a deep personal loss. Kasturbai, who was also imprisoned, as she had been along with Gandhi on many occasions, fell ill. On February 22, 1944, Kasturbai, the often silent heroine of India, died of acute bronchitis. Kasturbai had worked side by side with Gandhi on every political and spiritual movement. They had been married for 62 years. Gandhi was devastated. He became seriously ill from malaria, and Churchill, fearing damage to his own reputation, ordered Gandhi's release, which occurred on May 6, 1944. Although Linlithgow was certain Gandhi would die, he recovered after his release from prison.

THE SIMLA CONFERENCE

The war ended in 1945, and although the Allies were victorious, Britain lost its global political status. Churchill's term was over, and the new prime minister, Clement Atlee, made his top concern the granting of independence to India. He enlisted a new viceroy, Archibald Wavell, to enact this order. Viceroy Wavell released the nationalist leaders from prison and engaged them in negotiations at the Simla Conference in June 1945. Although not a delegate, Gandhi was also invited to the conference.

However, the plans for an independent India were deterred by Mohammad Ali Jinnah, leader of the Muslim League. He had desired to have the Muslims separated from the Hindus since the Government of India Act of 1935. His first action was to elect only Muslims from the Muslim League to the future government, because he felt that those in the Indian National Congress were too influenced by the Hindus. He greatly feared that the Hindu majority would suffocate the Muslims. He then sought to partition India and create a completely separate state for the Muslims, named Pakistan. He felt that separation would end their conflicts.

The Second Simla Conference began in March 1946, when Sir Stafford Cripps traveled to India to embark on more negotiations. No agreement could be reached between Nehru and Jinnah. It seemed that a partitioned India was an impossibility: it would tear apart Bengal and Punjab. India would be strong if united but, if partitioned, India and Pakistan would be weak. Nehru offered

Jinnah many concessions, but Jinnah would accept nothing short of a partitioning. When the conference concluded, it was decided that India needed a united leader for survival. Viceroy Wavell gave the responsibility of the head of government to Nehru. He offered Jinnah a high position and promised good faith. Jinnah refused any compromise and announced to the conference that on August 16, 1946, violent action would be taken that would continue until the Muslim community was granted its own nation.

THE MUSLIM AND HINDU WAR

Four days after the conference, on August 16, 1946, Jinnah held to his promise. Muslims began attacking Hindus in Calcutta, and thousands were killed and many more were wounded. The attacks also erupted in Bengal. The Hindus counterattacked and killed a massive number of Muslims in Bihar. Gandhi began to travel from town to town, conferring with Muslims and Hindus to try to bring peace. He was insulted by both sides. Many Muslims cursed him because he was Hindu, while Hindus denounced him for his kindness to the Muslims. He pleaded with Jinnah to concede to a united India.

FINAL ARRANGEMENTS WITH MOUNTBATTEN

Lord Mountbatten was the final viceroy of India. He was sent to make the final negotiations for independence and to assure that India was not in danger of civil war once the British quit India. He met with Gandhi, who talked to Mountbatten of the importance of a unified India. He then held a conference with Jinnah, who assured Mountbatten that if India were not partitioned, there would be a civil war.

Gandhi continued to try to bring peace between the Muslims and Hindus, without success, however. He met with Nehru and stressed that he must not give in to a partitioned India. Gandhi continually met with Jinnah. Jinnah was eventually offered Nehru's position of prime minister, as long as the battles would end and he conceded to a united India. Jinnah refused anything but his desire for the creation of Pakistan.

Eventually, Viceroy Mountbatten held a final conference for the plan of Indian independence. Nehru and the members of Congress could no longer take the battles between the Muslims and the Hindus. Tired from their struggles for independence, they gave in to Jinnah's demands. The viceroy set forth on the plans for an independent India and the creation of Pakistan. Mountbatten stayed in India for sometime after the day of independence to act as governor-general and help maintain order if necessary

INDIA GAINS ITS INDEPENDENCE

On August 15, 1947, India was finally granted independence from Britain. It was a day of long-awaited celebration. The long struggle of the nationalists had ended. India became the largest democracy in the world. On this day Pakistan was also partitioned from India and instated as an independent country. For some, it was a day of being uprooted or seeking refuge. Hindus evacuated the region now known as Pakistan for India, and Muslims fled India for Pakistan. Jawarharlal Nehru served as India's first prime minister. Soon after independence day, the leader of the untouchables, Dr. Bhimao Ramji Ambedkar, with some help from the Constituent Assembly, began drafting the constitution of India. The constitution contained standards of equality for all people, no matter what race, religion, or caste. It also implemented government directives for policies for the financial welfare of the people, workers' rights, and suitable health care.

THE ASSASSINATION OF GANDHI

On the day of independence, many saluted and hailed Gandhi for India's success. Gandhi did not rejoice. He was deeply saddened and spent the day fasting in atonement. He was very distraught over the partitioning of India, and the continued fighting between the Muslims and Hindus. Even as the two groups traveled to their new countries, the fighting continued well after the granting of independence. He traveled to Calcutta and Delhi to end the battles. Many feared for his safety, but he refused to be guarded. They felt he was in danger of assassination by extremist Muslims or Hindus. He further angered many Hindus by demanding that Pakistan be paid a fee owed to it by the Indian government. He fasted in Delhi and Calcutta until he successfully received written agreements that the fighting would cease. He often had many followers who fasted in support, including some of the remaining British policemen. The fasts worked very well in both situations.

On January 30, 1948, in Delhi, as Gandhi hurried to a prayer meeting, he was approached by the editor of a Hindu newspaper. The man's name was Nathuram Godse. He bent down as a sign of respect, as traditional custom calls for, and touched Gandhi's feet. Gandhi greeted him with a smile and joined his hands together. Godse quickly pulled his hands apart, withdrew a revolver disguised in his clothing, and shot Gandhi three times. Godse had once been a follower of Gandhi's and had even gone to

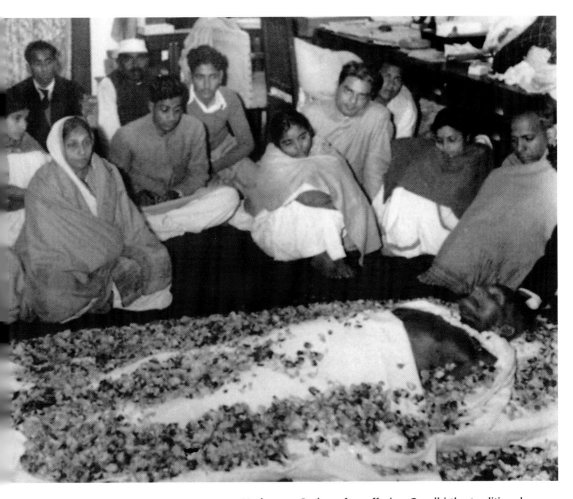

On January 30, 1948 Nathuram Godse, after offering Gandhi the traditional Hindu greeting of respect, shot the Mahatma three times. Gandhi's violent end sent millions of his followers into deep mourning. His petal-strewn body lies in state in New Delhi surrounded by relatives and close associates.

prison for his involvement. He killed Gandhi in the name of a radical Hindu group focusing on Brahman superiority. This quickly became a nationwide day of mourning for India and Pakistan. Gandhi's desire for peace came for the event of his death. Millions attended his funeral service to say good-bye to the father of their nation.

1600	Queen Elizabeth I grants the East India Company a royal charter
1603	Akbar officially grants the East India Company trading rights
1605	Death of Akbar and accession of Jahangir
1611	The East India Company establishes a factory in Masulipatam
1616	The East India Company establishes in Surat a second factory
1627	Death of Jahangir and accession of Shah Jahan
1631	Construction of the Taj Mahal
1639	The East India Company lays foundation for its first fort, Fort St. George, in Madras
1658	Aurangzeb usurps Shah Jahan and becomes Mughal emperor
1661	The British gain Bombay from the Portuguese
1664	Shivaji and the Marthas attack Surat
1674	Shivaji assumes the title of Chhatrapati, king of the Marthas
1680	Death of Shivaji
1682	Rebellion of Prince Akbar
1683	Aurangzeb begins war with the Marthas
1688	The East India Company engages in Child's War with the Mughal Empire
1689	Child's War ends
1707	Death of Aurangzeb; succession crisis and decline of Mughal Empire follows
1716	Farrukhsiyar grants the East India Company an imperial farman
1748	Beginning of French and English War in India
1749–1754	Carnatic Wars
1756	Siraj-ud-Daulah invades Calcutta; Black Hole of Calcutta
1757	Battle of Plassey
1760	Battle of Wandiwash
1763	Treaty of Paris ends French and English War
1765	The British gain Diwani Rights in Bengal, Bihar, and Orissa
1767–1769	First Mysore War
1773	The Regulating Act of 1773 passes; Warren Hastings appointed governor-general

1775–1782 First Martha War

1780–1784 Second Mysore War

1790–1792 Third Mysore War

1799 Fourth Mysore War

1803–1805 Second Martha War

1817–1818 Third Martha War; Pindari War

1839–1842 Afghan Wars

1845–1846 First Sikh War

1848–1849 Second Sikh War

1853 First railway laid in India, from Bombay to Thâne; first telegraph line goes in from Calcutta to Agra

1857 Mutiny of 1857

1858 India becomes a colony of the British Crown

1861 Indian Councils Act; Indian High Courts Act

1868 Beginning of railway expansion throughout India

1876 Queen Victoria is proclaimed empress of India

1885 First meeting of the Indian National Congress

1891 Indian Factory Act

1897 Plague in Bombay

1905 Attempt made to partition Bengal

1906 Formation of the Muslim League

1908 Newspaper Act

1912 The British capital is moved from Calcutta to Delhi

1913 Education Resolution of the Government of India

1916 Home Rule League founded; women's university established in Pune

1919 Rowlatt Acts evoke protest; Gandhi leads Congress in noncooperation movement; Amritsar massacre

1922 Civil disobedience movement

1923 Enactment of salt tax; Hindus and Muslims riot

1925 Reforms Inquiry Committee report

1929 Lord Irwin promises eventual dominion status for India; Congress gives year's notice of declaration of independence

1930 Congress declares India's independence; civil disobedience movement; salt march

1931 Gandhi attends Second Round Table Conference in England

1932 Suppression of independence movement; Third Round Table Conference

1933 Civil disobedience movement ends

1935 Government of India Act

1939 World War II begins; Britain assumes India's participation; Congress refuses unless independence promised

1942 Quit India Movement; members of Congress and Gandhi jailed

1944 Gandhi and Jinnah meet on Pakistan issue

1947 *June 3:* Lord Mountbatten announces plan for partition of India

August 15: India gains independence from Britain and is partitioned into India and Pakistan

1948 *January 30:* Mahatma Gandhi assasinated

September: Indian government troops are sent to Hyderabad

November: B. R. Ambedkar presents first draft of constitution to Constituent Assembly

1949 United Nations monitors cease-fire in Kashmir

September: Rupee devalued by 31 percent

November 26: Constitution of India adopted and signed

Basham, Al. *A Cultural History of India.* Delhi: Oxford University Press, 1997.

James, Lawrence. *The Rise and Fall of the British Empire.* New York: St. Martin's Press, 2000.

Malaspina, Ann. *Mahatma Gandhi and India's Independence in World History.* Berkeley Heights, N.J.: Enslow Publishers, 2000.

Martin, Christopher. *Mohandas Gandhi.* A&E Biography Series. Minneapolis: Lerner Publishing,

BOOKS:

Clément, Catherine. *Gandhi: The Power of Pacifism.* New York: Harry N. Abrams, 1996.

Cohn, Bernard. *Colonialism and Its Forms of Knowledge: The British in India.* Princeton, N.J.: Princeton University Press, 1996.

Dalton, Dennis, ed. *Mahatma Gandhi: Selected Political Writings.* Vol. 1. Indianapolis: Hackett Publishing, 1996.

Fowler, Michael Ross, and Julie Marie Bunck. *Law, Power and the Sovereign State.* University Park, Penn.: Pennsylvania State University Press, 1995.

Gandhi, Mohandas K. *Gandhi: An Autobiography: The Story of My Experiments with Truth.* Vol. 2. Boston: Beacon Press, 1993.

James, Lawrence. Raj: *The Making and Unmaking of British India.* New York: St. Martin's Press, 2000.

Keay, John. *India: A History.* New York: Grove Press, 2000.

Kipling, Rudyard. *The Jungle Book.* New York: Puffin Classics, 1995.

——. *The Second Jungle Book.* New York: Viking Press, 1987.

Moon, Penderel. *The Conquest and Dominion of India.* London: Duckworth Press, 1989.

Thoreau, Henry David. *Civil Disobedience.* Bedford, Mass.: Applewood Books, 2000.

WEB SITES:

www.albion.appstate.edu
www.elite.net/gurpal/
www.fordham.edu
www.historyofindia.com
www.memberstripod.com
www.sscnet.ucla.edu

Afghanistan
  and Afghan Wars, 63-65
  and Britain, 59
  and Marthas, 60
  and Sikh Wars, 66
Akbar (son of Aurangzeb), 13-15, 20,
  22, 118
Amritsar massacre, 95
Atlee, Clement, 113
Auckland, 65
Aurangzeb, 20-26, 62

Bahadur Shah (Prince Muzzaam), 27
Bengal
  and Britain, 58, 72
  and East India Company, 43-47, 50
  and Mutiny of 1857, 67-69
  and partition attempt, 79-80, 113
Bentinck, William, 63
Bihar, indigo growers from, 91-92, 94
"Black Hole of Calcutta," 44-45
Bombay
  and Britain, 59, 72
  and East India Company, 23-24, 26,
    27, 43
  and Marthan Wars, 60-61
British Commission, 98-99

Calcutta
  Black Hole of, 44-45
  and Britain, 59
  and East India Company, 26, 27,
    44-45
  and Siraj-ud-Daulah, 43-44
Carnatic Wars, 38-40
Charles II, King, 23, 25
Child's War, 25-26, 52
Christianity, and sepoys, 67-69, 71
Churchill, Winston, 109-110, 111,
  112-113
Civil disobedience, 89-90, 95, 96, 98-99,
  100, 101-103, 105, 106, 109-111
Civil liberties, 78, 81, 82, 91-92, 94-95,
  100, 105-106
Clive, Robert, 39, 40-41, 43, 44-46, 47,
  57, 58, 59

Columbus, Christopher, 9
Compagnie des Indes, 34-42, 47-49, 50
Company men, of East India Company,
  10, 11-12, 13, 24-25
Congress of Ministry, 107-108
Constitution, 115-116
Cornwallis, Charles, 54-56
Crown Colony, 71, 72-81

Dalhousie, Lord, 66
Dara Shikoh, 20
Deccan, 22, 24, 25
Delhi
  restoration of Mughal rule in, 69-70
  silent protest in, 95
Dominion status, 100, 111
Dupleix, Joseph-François, 35, 36, 38, 39,
  41-42, 48

East India Company
  and Afghan Wars, 63-65
  and Compagnie des Indes, 34-42,
    47-49
  and cultural impact on India, 76
  deconstruction of, 71, 72
  and *farman*, 14-15, 18, 19, 25, 26-29,
    30, 33, 34
  formation of, 9-13
  and Hastings, 59
  and Indian product and trade, 15-16
  and Marthan Wars, 60-62
  as military and economic power, 28,
    29, 30-49
  and Mutiny of 1857, 67-71, 72
  and Mysore, 50-57
  Parliament altering role of, 57
  and Russian phobia, 63-66
  and seizure of Madras, 19
  and Sikh Wars, 66-67
  and trade relationship with Mughal
    Empire, 13-29
Economy, colonial, 73-74
Education, 75, 77, 78
Elizabeth I, Queen, 9-10
English language, 77
Estado da India, 9

Farman, 14-15, 18, 19, 25, 26-29, 30, 33, 34
Farrukhsiyar, 27, 118
First Round Table Conference, 101
Fort St. George, 19
Fort William, 26, 43, 44
France, and India, 34-42, 47-49, 53
French and English War, 34-42, 47-49

Gaidilita, Rani, 103
Gandhi, Kasturbai, 84, 85, 89, 112
Gandhi, Mohandas, 82-92, 94-99
    assassination of, 116-117
    and civil disobedience, 89-90, 95, 96, 98-99, 101-103, 106, 109-111
    and early years, 84-85
    and Hindus and Muslims, 97-98, 114, 115, 116
    and independence, 83-84, 91, 101-105, 106, 111-113, 114, 116
    as lawyer, 85, 86-89
    as Mahatma, 91
    and marriage, 84, 85, 89, 112
    and noncooperation movement, 95-97, 111
    and Quit India Movement, 111-113
    and relations with Britain, 90
    and return to India, 91
    and salt march, 101-103
    and search for truth, 83-84, 86, 88, 89-90, 106, 109
    and Second Round Table conference, 103-105
    in South Africa, 86-90
    and studies in London, 85-86
    and textile workers, 91-92, 94
    and untouchables, 105-106
    and World War I, 94
    and World War II, 109, 110-111
Godse, Nathuram, 116-117
Government, colonial, 72-73, 74-76, 78-79, 80-81, 82, 105-106, 107-108, 111
    See also Indian National Congress; Muslim League
Government of India Act, 107-108, 113
Gurkhas, and Mutiny of 1857, 69

Guru Tegh Bahadur, 21-22

Haidar Ali, 52-53, 54
Hastings, Warren, 53, 57-59, 60-61
Hawkins, William, 16
Hedges, William, 25
Hindus
    and Afghan Wars, 65
    and Gandhi, 91, 97-98, 114, 115, 116
    and Indian National Congress, 81
    and Mughals, 13, 20, 22
    Muslims separate from, 108, 113
    Muslims united with, 95, 97-98
    as sepoys, 67-69, 71
    and untouchables, 105-106, 115
    and violence against Muslims, 114, 115, 116
Hyderabad, 48, 51-52, 54

Independence, 82, 100-117
    declaration of, 100
    See also Gandhi, Mohandas
Independence day, 115, 116
Independents, of East India Company, 24-25
India
    Britain's conquering of, 45-47, 50-71
    Britain's emergence into, 7, 9-29
    and independence, 82, 100-117
    westernization of as British Crown Colony, 71, 72-81
    See also Gandhi, Mohandas
India National Congress Party, 108
Indian National Congress, 78-79, 80, 82, 89, 91, 95, 96, 98, 99, 100, 108-111, 112, 113
Indians, in East India Company, 12-13
Indonesian spice trade, 9, 15
Interlopers, of East India Company, 24-25

Jafar, Mir, 45, 46-47
Jahangir (Salim), 16, 17-18, 118
James I, King, 17, 18
Jinnah, Mohammad Ali, 108, 112, 113-114, 115

Jodhpur, 22

Kabul, Afghanistan, 65
Kanhoji Angria, 26
Karnataka, 38-40, 56
Khan, Shaista, 25
Khan Abdul Ghafar, 103
Kipling, Rudyard, 76
Koh-i-noor diamond, 63, 67

Lucknow, 70

Madras
    and Britain, 59, 72
    and East India Company, 19, 27, 36,
        37, 39, 48, 50
    and France, 36, 48
Martha-Pindari War, 62
Marthas
    and Cornwallis, 54
    and East India Company, 26, 33, 40,
        43, 59
    and Marthan Wars, 59-63
    and Mughals, 22, 23, 32
    and Mysore, 52, 53
Meerut rebellion, 69-70
Mewar, 22
Mountbatten, Lord, 114, 115
Mughal Empire
    dissolution of, 31-34, 34, 35
    restoration of in Delhi, 69-70
    and trade relationship with East
        India Company, 13-29
    tribute payments to, 58
Muslim League, 80, 82, 99, 100, 108,
    112, 113
Muslims
    and Gandhi, 97-98, 114, 115, 116
    Hindus united with, 95, 97-98
    and Indian National Congress, 80-81
    and Mughals, 13, 20-22
    and Muslim League, 80, 81, 82, 99,
        100, 108, 112, 113
    and Pakistan, 113-114, 115, 116
    and separation from Hindus, 108, 113

    as sepoys, 67-69, 71
    and violence against Hindus, 114,
        115, 116
Mutiny of 1857, 67-71, 72
Mysore Wars, 50-57, 59

Nationalists, 82, 95, 96, 98, 99
    See also Independence
Nehru, Jawaharlal, 100, 103, 104, 106,
    113-114, 115
Nizam Ali, 52
Noncooperation movement, 95-97, 111
Northern Circars, 48

Pakistan, 113-114, 115, 116
Partition, 113-114, 115, 116
Peshawar, 64
Peshwa, 60, 62, 70
Pindaris, 62
Plassey, Battle of, 45-47
Principalities, 32-34, 38, 60
Pune, 60, 61, 62, 70
Punjab, 63, 66-67, 113

Quit India Movement, 111-113

Railways, 74
Regulating Act of 1773, 57
Roe, Sir Thomas, 16-18, 19
Romantic period, 47
Roosevelt, Franklin, 111
Rowlatt Acts, 95
Russia, and East India Company, 63-66

Salt, taxation of, 74
    and salt march, 101-103
Sambhaji, 22
Satyagraha, 90
Second Round Table Conference,
    103-105
Sepoys, 28, 33, 35, 36, 40, 65
    and Mutiny of 1857, 67-71
Shah Jahan (Khurram), 18-20, 118
Sharia, law of, 20
Shivaji, 22, 23, 63

Sikhs
    and Afghan Wars, 63-65
    and Marthan Wars, 61
    and Mughals, 20-22
    and Mutiny of 1857, 69
    and Sikh Wars, 66-67
Simla Conference, 113-114
Sind, 65
Siraj-ud-Daulah, 43-47
Speech, suppression of, 78
Stockholders, of East India Company,
    10-11
Swadeshi Movement, 80

Taj Mahal, 18
Taxation, 74
Textile workers, 91-92, 94

Third Round Table Conference, 105
Thoreau, Henry David, 89
Tippu Sultan, 52, 53-56

Untouchables, 105-106, 115

Vasco Da Gama, 9
Victoria, Queen, 67, 74-76
Vijaydurg, 43

Wandiwash, Battle of, 49
Watson, Charles, 43, 44
Wellesley, Richard, 56, 61, 62
Women, role of, 75
World War II, 108-111

Yale, Elihu, 24

page:

6:	Courtesy of the U.S. Central Intelligence Agency	58:	Hulton Archive by Getty Images
8:	Courtesy of the U.S. Central Intelligence Agency	64:	Hulton Archive by Getty Images
		68:	Hulton Archive by Getty Images
11:	Hulton Archive by Getty Images	73:	Associated Press, AP
17:	Hulton Archive by Getty Images	77:	Hulton Archive by Getty Images
21:	Hulton Archive by Getty Images	83:	Associated Press, AP
23:	Hulton Archive by Getty Images	87:	Associated Press, AP
31:	© Corbis	92:	Associated Press, AP
37:	Hulton Archive by Getty Images	97:	Hulton Archive by Getty Images
41:	Hulton Archive by Getty Images	101:	Hulton Archive by Getty Images
46:	Hulton Archive by Getty Images	104:	Associated Press, AP
51:	Hulton Archive by Getty Images	107:	Hulton Archive by Getty Images
55:	Hulton Archive by Getty Images	110:	Associated Press, AP
		117:	Associated Press, AP

ABOUT THE AUTHOR

JENNIFER M. BREEN is a writer and freelance editor. She is also a teacher in the FOUNDATIONS program in Philadelphia. She has her B.A. in English literature from Rosemont College, Rosemont, Pennsylvania.